SIR HALLEY STEWART TRUST: LECTURES

I0127583

Volume 3

FROM CHAOS
TO CONTROL

FROM CHAOS
TO CONTROL

NORMAN ANGELL

Routledge
Taylor & Francis Group

LONDON AND NEW YORK

First published in 1933 by George Allen & Unwin Ltd.

This edition first published in 2025
by Routledge
4 Park Square, Milton Park, Abingdon, Oxon OX14 4RN

and by Routledge
605 Third Avenue, New York, NY 10158

Routledge is an imprint of the Taylor & Francis Group, an informa business

British Library Cataloguing in Publication Data
A catalogue record for this book is available from the British Library

ISBN: 978-1-032-88942-9 (Set)
ISBN: 978-1-032-87865-2 (Volume 3) (hbk)
ISBN: 978-1-032-87870-6 (Volume 3) (pbk)
ISBN: 978-1-003-53489-1 (Volume 3) (ebk)

DOI: 10.4324/9781003534891

Publisher's Note
The publisher has gone to great lengths to ensure the quality of this reprint but points out that some imperfections in the original copies may be apparent.

Disclaimer
The publisher has made every effort to trace copyright holders and would welcome correspondence from those they have been unable to trace.

This book is a re-issue originally published in 1933. The language used and views portrayed are a reflection of its era and no offence is meant by the Publishers to any reader by this re-publication.

THE
HALLEY STEWART TRUST

★

FOUNDED 15TH DECEMBER 1924
FOR RESEARCH TOWARDS THE CHRISTIAN IDEAL IN ALL
SOCIAL LIFE.

The objects of the Trust are *in general*:

To advance religion; to advance education; to relieve poverty; to promote other Charitable purposes beneficial to the community, and *in particular*:

1. To assist in the discovery of the best means by which "the mind of Christ" may be applied to extending the Kingdom of God by the prevention and removal of human misery;

2. To assist in the study of our Lord's life and teaching in their explicit and implicit application to the social relationships of man;

3. To express the mind of Christ in the realization of the Kingdom of God upon earth and in a national and a world-wide brotherhood;

For example:

*For every Individual, by furthering such favourable oppor-
tunities of education, service, and leisure as shall enable him
or her most perfectly to develop the body, mind, and spirit:*

*In all Social Life, whether domestic, industrial, or
national, by securing a just environment, and*

*In International Relationships, by fostering good will
between all races, tribes, peoples, and nations so as to secure
the fulfilment of the hope of "peace on earth";*

4. To provide fees for a Lecture or Lectures annually and
   prizes for essays or other written compositions, and to
   pay for their publication and distribution;

5. To provide, maintain, and assist Lectures and Research
   work in Social, Economic, Psychological, Medical,
   Surgical, or Educational subjects;

6. To make grants to Libraries;

7. To assist publications exclusively connected with the
   objects of the Trust (not being newspapers or exclusively denominational);

8. To make grants to and co-operate with Societies,
   Organizations, and Persons engaged in the furtherance
   of Charitable objects similar to the objects of the Trust;

9. To use the foregoing and any such other methods,
   whether of a like nature or not, as are lawful and reasonable and appropriate for the furtherance of the objects
   of the Trust.

The income of the Trust may not be used for dogmatic
theological or ecclesiastical purposes other than the cult of
the Science of God as manifest in man in the Son of Man
in the person and teaching of Our Lord, "The Word of
God," Who "liveth and abideth forever."

HALLEY STEWART LECTURE, 1932

FROM CHAOS TO CONTROL

by

NORMAN ANGELL

LONDON

GEORGE ALLEN & UNWIN LTD

MUSEUM STREET

FIRST PUBLISHED IN 1933
SECOND IMPRESSION 1935

PRINTED IN GREAT BRITAIN BY
UNWIN BROTHERS LTD., WOKING

AUTHOR'S NOTE

THESE five chapters represent the expansion of notes used in the delivery of the Halley Stewart Lectures for 1932–1933.

As the lectures were not read from manuscript, but delivered extempore from notes, I have not hesitated to add a good deal of material which might have appeared in the form of footnotes, but which, for the purposes of this book, I have preferred to include in the body of the chapters.

CONTENTS

		PAGE
I.	THE PATIENT AND THE DOCTORS	15
II.	THE DISBELIEF IN ECONOMIC SANITA-TION	59
III.	DO WE KNOW WHAT WE WANT?	100
IV.	THE CONDITIONS OF SUCCESSFUL PLANNING	127
V.	WHERE EDUCATION FALLS SHORT	172
	INDEX	213

FROM CHAOS TO CONTROL

I

THE PATIENT AND THE DOCTORS

LAST year's Halley Stewart Lecture dealt with the World's Economic Crisis and the Way of Escape. To suggestions concerning the way of economic escape contributed six men, who have greater authority to make suggestion to that end than any other six men in the world.[1]

You can imagine the diffidence, therefore, with which I follow them. And I should not follow them at all if the phase of the problem with which I am proposing to deal were the purely economic phase. But it is not. It is related to the problem which they attacked, and the one which I propose to discuss must be solved if their remedies are ever to be applied. But it is a quite distinct problem. It is that of the psychology of popular understanding, of the nature of the public mind in relation to the technical problems discussed by last year's lecturers; a problem of education, of politics. And as it is even more important in the case of a series of lectures than in the case of a single one, to know clearly what the theme is I had better, at the

[1] *The World's Economic Crisis and the Way of Escape*, by Sir Arthur Salter, Sir Josiah Stamp, J. Maynard Keynes, Sir Basil Blackett, Henry Clay, Sir W. H. Beveridge. Halley Stewart Lecture, 1931. George Allen & Unwin, London.

very beginning, like Luther, nail my thesis to the church door.

It is this: That it serves little purpose to find the way of escape if those who are to tread it do not believe it to be the way of escape, and refuse to follow it. The problem which confronts our modern democracies is the problem of choosing between a great many different remedies that are offered them, often between rival and mutually exclusive remedies, sometimes based upon highly technical considerations, of the merits of which it is often extremely difficult for the layman to judge. One has only to recall the debates which during the last year or two have raged over the various kinds of Protection and the various kinds of Free Trade; between advocates of inflation and deflation; spending and saving; a gold standard, a bimetallic one and a variety of managed currency schemes; more control and less; Socialism and Individualism; Communism and Private Property. . . . The list is endless; and it must seem to the patient that the doctors are in most violent disagreement. And if the problem for the layman is to know how to choose, the problem for the expert adviser is not only, and not first, to find the way of escape; it is first to enable those for whom the way of escape is designed, and who are travelling in other directions, to see that it is indeed the right road. If they are unable for any reason to do this, it is as though, in order to save a vessel from shipwreck in difficult waters, great and exhaustive care were taken to write down all the true sailing directions and then to give the book containing those directions into the hands of seamen who could not read.

Yet this is an aspect of the problem which is curiously neglected. We seem to assume that if only someone could find the cure for our diseases we should at once see that it *was* the cure and apply it. We ask for leaders and leadership. But if the right course which the leader would have the multitudes take happens to be the course which the multitude sincerely believes to be the wrong one, they will immediately declare that he is no leader but a misleader. Inevitably in a democracy the leader is he who expresses existing convictions in the most vivid way, who possesses, as someone puts it, "the common mind to an uncommon degree."

How can it be otherwise? The convictions of the multitudes—and on certain points like the desirability of organizing the world on a nationalist basis there is overwhelming agreement—are sincere convictions. They are, as we know, sometimes disastrously erroneous; but they are also disastrously honest. One can imagine people pretending to beliefs they don't hold hypocritically and insincerely for some purpose of advantage to themselves. But one cannot imagine whole nations maintaining a pretence for generation after generation for the purpose of making themselves poor and depriving themselves of their property. No. The Nationalisms, the Protectionisms, the Mercantilisms and all the other

B

fallacies which rack Europe and create the chaos are sincerely held fallacies. They are, to these multitudes, the truth; and the prophet who denies them shall be stoned.

So leaders cannot help us much if they merely lead more forcefully and more quickly in the wrong direction. The prophets can only help, to the degree that they are able to show that errors sincerely held as the truth are not the truth; and thus make possible the perception of the right way.

It was not the task of the lecturers last year to attack that particular problem of under-standing. Their task was to find the economic solution. Mine is to find how that solution may be made acceptable to the public who have to apply it; how the common man may be made to see that it is indeed the solution.

The problem is, of course, intimately related to the problem of democracy as a whole. If the multitudes cannot distinguish in the policies presented to them between folly and wisdom, science and quackery, the efficient democratic control of our increasingly complicated economic apparatus becomes impossible. But I shall try to show that there is no real escape by the road of dictatorship; that democracy is inevitable in the sense that ultimately the dominant attitudes and ways of thought on things like nationalism will determine the kind of society which we have, despite dictatorships or other supposed alter-natives.

I shall try to show further that the collapse of the democratic method is not inevitable; that it is due largely to the failure of organized education to prepare those in its charge to understand the new kind of society which the last half-century or so has brought into being.

And finally, that this failure of education is, in its turn, an avoidable failure, and that it is due largely to the fact that education simply has not set before itself very consciously or definitely the aim of enabling the mass of men to understand the mechanism of their new society, the relation of human nature and its management thereto.

The special part of the task to which I propose to devote this afternoon is to show the fact and degree of failure. For this is one of those cases in which it is true to say that the essence of truth is degree; that our judgment of what is necessary and what must be done will depend upon our realization of the extent and character of the failure of understanding. You see I am not suggesting that the failure of understanding is occasional and slight, but constant, deep and fundamental, although, tragically enough, I do not believe that it is due to any inherent defect of the average man's capacity. I believe it to be a failure that can be remedied.

One of last year's lecturers did indeed refer to the particular difficulty I am putting before you. In his address, Sir Josiah Stamp said:

If one devotes one's time to setting out a series of remedies and solutions, they are nearly always unacceptable. People are so impatient of anything unpalatable that their minds are practically inhibited from accepting them outright. There must be an easier path ! It is only when inevitability is borne in upon people's minds by a process of elimination that some of the remedies can possibly be accepted with anything like intellectual conviction.

And I thought it was an apt commentary on this that in the closing lecture Sir William Beveridge, summing up the whole, in an answer to the question "What would a dictator do if he had absolute power ?" said this:

I am going to ask you, Sir Halley, as you sit there, presiding over us, kindly to imagine yourself to be a miracle-working spirit, able to do or get done all that I think should be done in the world to make economic life more stable. What tasks should I give you, in what order?

I have no doubt about the first two tasks.

First, you would go and tell all the governments concerned to drop here and now the whole business of war debts and reparations. Those international obligations arising out of the war are just a continuation of war. They block the way to international co-operation, and are among the worst rigidities of our economic system. They have no moral sanction; they are not like other obligations. Psychologically and economically they are evil.

Second, you would go and tell all the governments from me that they have to abolish tariffs, not of course suddenly, for that, in high tariff countries, would cause devastation, but under a scheme by which automatically year by year, throughout the world, all tariff walls would slowly sink back into the ground. With them would go all systems of export bounties, sur-taxes and the rest, by which one country tries to get richer at the expense of others. One might need a twenty-year plan to allow time for the industry of each country to readjust itself and put the human race in a position to make the best of Nature's gifts throughout the world.

Those would be your first two tasks.

I have drawn your attention to this detail of the previous lectures in order to make my first point about the disagreement of the doctors and the puzzlement of the public. You may argue: Is it not first for the doctors to agree, since if they did the public would follow the road indicated readily enough? I do not believe that this is true, for where all the doctors of any scientific qualification do agree the public do not follow.

Here are two points, those indicated by Sir William Beveridge—two very important and fundamental points—on which the doctors are in entire agreement; and the public do not follow the way indicated; they follow the contrary way.

Indeed, about these proposals of Sir William Beveridge three things at least could be said:

First, that not only the six experts who lectured here, but all the experts in the world, are broadly in agreement that those things ought to be done.[1]

[1] The Basle Committee, composed of representatives of the Chief Central Banks of the World and presided over by the representative of the Federal Reserve System of the United States, reported as follows:

"In recent years the world has been endeavouring to pursue two contradictory policies in permitting the development of an international financial system which involves the annual payment of large sums by debtor to creditor countries, while at the same time putting obstacles in the way of the free movement of goods. So long as these obstacles remain, such movements of capital must necessarily throw the world's financial balance out of equilibrium. Financial remedies alone will be powerless to restore the world's economic prosperity until there is a radical change in this policy of obstruction,

Secondly, that though the doing of those things will not of itself provide the way of escape, if they are not done any remedy which is applied will work very imperfectly or not at all.

And thirdly, that not merely are those indispensable steps not being taken, not merely is that way of escape not being followed, but every nation in the world, including this nation, supported in most cases by the overwhelming mass of popular opinion, is travelling in the exactly opposite direction.

Which brings us to what is my first and last proposition: that much of the economic disease from which we suffer is due to a failure to grasp the very few but very important truths upon which

and international commerce—on which depends the progress of civilization—is allowed to resume its natural development."

". . . We think it is essential that before the period of prolongation of credits recommended by the London Conference comes to an end (February 1927), they should give the world the assurance that international political relations are established on such basis of mutual confidence, which is the *sine qua non* of economic recovery, as will not emperil the maintenance of her financial stability.

". . . in order to revive demand and thus to put an end to the continued downward movement of prices—which is enclosing both debtor and creditor countries in a vicious circle of depression—it is essential that the normal process of investment of fresh capital should be resumed, with a well-defined economic purpose in view—namely, an increase in the purchasing power of the world."

And the Committee warns us:

"Time is short. The body of the world's commerce—whose vitality is already low—has suffered a severe shock in one of its chief members. This has resulted in partial paralysis which can only be cured by restoring the free circulation of money and of goods. We believe that this can be accomplished; but only if the governments of the world will realize the responsibility that rests upon them and will take prompt measures to re-establish confidence. Their action alone can restore it."

all the economic doctors are agreed; that if we had avoided what is avoidable the remainder of the problem would be much more manageable; that there is nothing inherently difficult in understanding the reason for the course advised by all the economists; and that the most urgent thing is to discover what stands in the way of that popular understanding. In that discovery lies the greatest hope of immediate alleviation. It is in any case indispensable, in that so long as we do not make it and persist in rejecting the very first rules of economic health, no treatment, no operation on the body politic, can succeed.

To reduce the question to still narrower terms by way of illustration: Why did it take Europe fifteen years to do at long last in that matter of Reparations what it might have done at once? Why does American public opinion refuse to take a course which every instructed person knows will have to be taken ultimately?

You will appreciate, of course, that in choosing the problem of Debts and Reparations I do so, not with the idea of suggesting that they are the sole or even the major cause of the chaos, but as illustrating the kind of failure of understanding, of popular confusion which confronts us. If we can understand the reason for the failure of the public mind in this respect, it will certainly help us to understand its failure in other respects.

The most recent example of this attitude of the ordinary voter to the conditions of recovery indicated by Sir William Beveridge is, of course, that furnished by the United States this last month or two. At the Presidential election both parties were compelled, on pain of rejection by the voters, to appear at least to favour this policy: (1) That there should be no cancellation or even reduction of debts; (2) That there should be no discussion with the debtors as a group; (3) That no connection between debts and reparations should be discussed; (4) That in any World Economic Conference, debts, reparations and tariffs were to be excluded. Congress has overwhelmingly reflected this general line by the attitude of individual members. It is true to say to-day that whatever a member's private opinion as to the advisability of debt cancellation or reduction may be, he cannot, if he values his political life at all, stand for that policy.[1]

The fate of Herriot is warning of what happens to even the most powerful of statesmen who challenge the popular views on such matters. You have in America at present this situation: on the one side practically every competent economist, every serious student of the subject, every banker of international experience, taking the view that at this juncture America's best interests demand a line of policy running directly counter to that indicated above, and on the other side all the politicians dependent upon popular

[1] Since the date of these lectures, and since the Presidential election, the American administration has considerably modified this policy, as the British Government modified its policy on Reparations after the election of 1918.

support standing by the policy just outlined. There are not a dozen members of the House of Representatives, not half a dozen Senators who dare plainly and unequivocally support the views upon which every serious student of the subject is agreed. For a politician so to do would be the end of him. And the view which no politician dare express for fear of public wrath happens to be not merely the expert view but the self-evidently true view. The popular view flouts arithmetic, flouts obvious fact; and the American case comes, furthermore, after fifteen years of European experience of exactly the same character of difficulties in the Reparations problem, of nations and governments refusing during those years to take a course which they have been obliged in the end to take and which, if they had taken early, doing at first what it was evident they would be compelled to do at last, would have saved the world an amount of loss and misery only comparable to that of the war itself.

We in Europe have no right, of course, to be in the least degree complacent, in view of the history of the Reparations claims, which for thirteen years made infinitely more difficult the already difficult economic and financial situation of Europe. If the governments of Europe had done early, immediately after the war, what in any case they were compelled to do at long last; if, that is, the public had understood the point which every expert tried to make clear, fourteen years of time might have been gained in applying necessary measures. The disease from which we suffer would have had nothing like the extent and intensity that it has.

Let us see what the point was—the point which it took the Allies some twelve or fourteen years to see—and which happens to be precisely the same point which now confronts America in the matter of the debts.

Just after the war a British commission, assisted by a great British banker, assessed Germany's "capacity to pay" at £24,000 million— that is to say, to make annual payments which capitalized would about represent that sum. Experts immediately pointed out that as all the gold in Germany would only amount to about one-hundredth part of this sum (even if it were in practice possible to take Germany's gold) the remainder—99 per cent. of the claim— would have to be paid in goods or services; by the expansion, that is, of Germany's exports. Were the Allies prepared to see the markets of the world so flooded with German goods? They were not. There was to be no German dumping, and any sign of it would be met by tariffs. Germany must pay, "in money, not goods."

I remember trying to put the case to certain members of the House of Commons who were clamouring for settlement in those terms. "We don't want Germany's goods," said they in effect, "we don't want Germany's gold; we want her money—the money that she is spending in her night clubs and on her extravagant public build-ings."

One member proposed to send a small army to Germany (this was just after the war) and collect the money in motor trucks and bring it to London. I asked him what he would do with it there. It would necessarily be paper money since all the gold in Germany could only pay about 1 per cent. of what we were claiming. But German paper money is no use in England (any more than English money is of use in the United States). Neither butcher nor baker, nor income-tax collector will accept it. German money is only of use in Germany, where indeed it will buy German goods. But those goods were not to be exported, must not leave the country, that is, or the Allied tariffs would go up to keep them out. I pointed out at the time that this plan of the British M.P. seemed to suggest that having got this German "money" and finding that it won't buy anything in Britain, we should all have to emigrate to Germany, and there drink German beer till the Reparations were exhausted.

It is an amazing fact in psychology that the "money illusion," as Professor Irving Fisher has called it, should so bemuse our minds that something which is in fact completely self-evi-dent, which it does not require any knowledge at all of technical economics to grasp, which a savage thinking in terms of goods, not money, would see immediately, escaped the understanding of all the nations for fourteen years—if indeed the public sees it yet.

From the beginning we ruled gold out of it: if we had taken every pair of earrings from Germany we could have got only a tiny fraction of what we were claiming. We did not want her goods or services. Then what remains? And to that question the public—the British and the French—went on parrot-like saying "MONEY." But the "money" would be *German* money, of no value anywhere but in *Germany*; a claim upon *German* goods or services, which we refused to take. We could not see, or we refused to see, that to go on saying "Pay, but we shall keep out your goods," is exactly equivalent to saying (as a German proverb puts it) "You must wash me, but you must not make me wet."

We had to choose between these courses: One was to make arrangement for accepting payment in specified goods or services; arranging, for instance, for Germany to rebuild the devastated areas with German labour and material. The Germans proposed and the French rejected this course. As an alternative to this we could so lower tariffs that normal international trade would be largely increased, so that Germany could pour into Allied countries, or into neutral countries, a larger amount of goods than she had been doing in the past, and to that extent, to the extent, that is, of her excess of exports over imports, could pay Reparations. If we were not prepared to accept this increase of German foreign trade, then plainly we had to surrender our claims for great Reparation payments. But we would do neither the one nor the other. Like children in a nursery we went on demanding that Germany pay while taking such action that it became physically impossible for her to pay. We kept on mixing our moral indignation with a question of physical possibility. "*How* can we pay if you cannot take our goods? Tell us *how?*" the Germans in effect kept on asking. And the Allies retorted: "Did you not cause the war? Did you not destroy the houses of Northern France? And now you don't want to pay."

And that is as far as we got.

Mr. Winston Churchill has vividly recalled the situation in his book on the World Crisis. Speaking of the line of reasoning just summarized, he says:

These arguments were unseasonable. Their mere statement exposed the speaker to a charge of being pro-German or at best a weakling. Not only the ordinary electors, but experts of all kinds, financial and economic, as well as business men and politicians, showed themselves unconsciously or wilfully blind to the stubborn facts (p. 46).

He himself would not accept the twelve hundred million a year fairy story, and indicates the technique by which the statesman, while adhering to the facts, may satisfy the popular demand for pleasing fiction. He writes:

I held firmly to the Treasury estimate when I faced the electors of Dundee. I dressed it up as well as possible. "We will make them pay an indemnity." (Cheers.) "We will make them pay a large indemnity." (Cheers.) "They exacted from France a large indemnity in 1870. We will make them pay ten times as much." (Prolonged cheers.) "(200 millions × 10 = 2,000 millions)." Everybody was delighted. It was only the next day that the figures began to be scrutinized. Then came a hectoring telegram from an important Chamber of Commerce. "Haven't you left out a nought in your indemnity figures?" The local papers gibbered with strident claims. Twelve thousand millions, fifteen thousand millions were everywhere on the lips of men and women who the day before had been quite happy with two thousand millions, and were not anyhow going to get either for themselves. However, adding under daily pressure "Of course, if we can get more, all the better," I stuck to my two thousand millions (p. 47).

Other writers of this time were reminding us, however, of the morass into which the popular misunderstanding was leading the nation. Mr. J. A. Spender wrote:

Is it really necessary that the whole world should be kept in suspense and its trade paralysed by maintaining vast claims which all instructed men know cannot be met, and, if they could be met, would be rejected by the claimants? Must we go on, year after year, verifying from costly experience what has now become self-evident? There was some excuse for ignorance in 1919. The idea of vast payments being made from one nation to others was a new one to the modern world, and the small sum exacted from France after the Franco-German War offered no analogies.

It is now more than ten years since the American economists, Professors Bass and Moulton, of the University of Chicago, wrote:

What hope is there for the world so long as the leading Premiers of Allied countries admit that Germany can pay only with goods which none of the Allied nations are willing to receive, and give

support to their Parliaments in framing tariff measures designed
to prevent German exports, at the same time insist that recal-
citrant Germany must meet the Reparation obligation to the last
farthing and the last sou? What hope is there for the world so
long as most of the leading students of international finance and
economics, who recognize the fundamental illusion in Reparations
and Allied debts, will frankly discuss the subject in undertones
and in inner offices? What hope is there for the world when
statesmen and financiers alike, while lacking the courage to tell
the truth about Reparations and inter-Allied debts, insist that
nothing can be done as a practical matter, "however desirable
it might be from an economic point of view," because the people
will not be satisfied to give up the supposed advantages of Reparations and debt payments? If ever there was a time for leadership
in a campaign of enlightenment on the fundamentals of international economics it is now. If ever there was a time when the
truth is needed to set men free, it is now. If ever there was a
time when evasion and concealment were political virtues, it
is *not* now.

Compare this situation in Britain and Europe
twelve or thirteen years ago to the present situation in America over debts. I have just come back
from America where this point of the debts was
subject to a nation-wide canvass, a nation-wide
discussion in the shape of a Presidential election.
It was a particularly good time to judge how the
public and the politicians (who were making an
intensive and shrewd study of what the voters
were feeling) were behaving in respect of the
recommendations of the experts. In some notes
made during and just after the election, I find
that the emphasis of the observations is centred
repeatedly on the fact that public understanding
of the Debts question in America is to-day at the

same stage that the European understanding of
the Reparations question was fourteen years ago.
That is to say, the public in America to-day sees
no connection whatever between the tariff and
the payment of debt; it still fails completely to
understand that if the Debts are to be paid by
Europe, America must somehow manage to
increase her imports. To-day in America, nine
thousand, nine hundred and ninety-nine out of
ten thousand ordinary business men would deny
emphatically that the amount of America's imports, or America's tariffs, have anything whatever
to do with Europe's capacity to pay the Debts.
The American is, of course, vaguely aware that
all Britain's remaining gold would only pay a
fraction of what she owes. Yet he insists that
she must pay "in money"—the only money she
possesses outside gold being British money, which
has no value in America, and can only be used
for the purchase of British goods which the
tariff shuts out. He does not relate the one fact
to the other.

By way of an attempt to bring home the nature
of the problem, I have betimes suggested to
Americans a plan by which Britain could completely pay her debt to America, relieve the
American taxpayer of an equivalent amount in
taxes, and avoid all transfer difficulties. Let Great
Britain in future build the American navy, and
supply all the military equipment that America
may need. The debt would be paid, not in
money, but in the delivery each year of thirty or

forty million pounds worth of military material. The American taxpayer would be relieved of that amount of taxes. (The great argument in America at present is that if Britain does not find the money the American taxpayer will be compelled to do so in order to pay interest on the bonds by means of which the money originally was raised.) The money the American taxpayer is now obliged to find for the navy could be applied to other purposes—purchase of motor-cars and radio sets—expanding those trades and so taking up ultimately the displaced labour of the American shipyards. Britain would not have to go into the exchange market to sell sterling, and still further disorganize her currency, injure her capacity to buy American goods and bring down the price of such American products as wheat and cotton. It is really a great scheme and gets over most of our difficulties. But in making the proposal I did not suppose for one moment that there was the faintest chance of its being accepted.

The American fails as completely to see that the transfer problem is the crux of the matter, as we failed to see it when we rampaged fourteen years ago for Germany to pay twenty-four thousand million sterling. All mention of the transfer problem is carefully excluded from the popular newspaper clamour about Debts. To-day, after fourteen years of the discussion of the Reparations, the Debts remain, for the great American public, a simple problem of British morality and honour. Day after day the Hearst Press still harps on the one refrain: "Is it or is it not true that the money was loaned to Britain, and that she promised to repay it? Honest people pay their debts and fulfil their obligations." And that's all.

Over his own signature Mr. Hearst writes:

Every corner grocery man knows that he would go into bankruptcy if he cancelled all the accounts which are owed him.

None of the banks practise the debt cancellation which these international bankers and their President are advocating for the American people. Go around to any bank and try to get your debt to the bank *cancelled* or *reduced* or revised *downward* or anything but *paid*.

No indeed, what is good for the goose is *not* good for the gander, and America is surely the goose all right, and a goosed goose at that, if it submits to Mr. Hoover's plan for debt cancellation by means of a moratorium.

Mr. Hearst's notion of economics and of international finance are, of course, extremely important for several reasons, not all equally obvious. Mr. Hearst in America (like Lord Beaverbrook in England) is the master of a whole chain of newspapers. Views of life like those just quoted are carried with all the powerful suggestibility which the modern newspaper can exercise simultaneously to perhaps a hundred organs scattered across the vast North American continent. To the reader in New York and Boston, in Chicago, on the Pacific Coast, and in the Southern States, he suggests that the rules which govern the economic conduct of the corner grocery man are the rules appropriate to nations. The appeal is the more powerful because that is how the layman usually does think of the economic relations of States (as witness the centuries during which the fallacy which economists call mercantilism has dominated the policy of nations). Economists may protest, but they have not always the gift of clarity; and where the academic economist can reach ten minds, Mr. Hearst can reach a million. He can dismiss economists as long-haired theorists, and most of his readers will agree. The suggestion that it is the action of America herself which largely makes the Debts unpayable simply does not get home, because the average American, like the average educated man of all countries, cannot follow the simplest, the most elementary, the most self-evident fact about the financial and economic apparatus which feeds and clothes us. It is an interesting comment on the way in which modern education prepares the voting millions, who make and unmake governments, who send the world to war and make the treaties of peace, to understand the nature of the world in which they live, and by votes, direct and manage. One is not surprised to find an authority like Mr. Frank Vanderlip, former President of the National City Bank of New York, the foremost banking institution in America, in an article in *The Saturday Evening Post*, describing America (although he could as truthfully include any people in Europe) as "a nation of economic illiterates." The country, he says, simply does not understand general economic truths, despite its industrial capacity. He quotes as an example the acceptance speech of Vice-President Curtis, who cited the increase in the amount of notes outstanding, as proof that the hoarding of currency was declining; it being evidence, of course, that it was increasing. Incidentally, Mr. Vanderlip calculates that the losses to stockholders during the slump have been three times what America spent fighting the World War. The percentage of decline in the value of securities has been greater than that in the South Sea Bubble. He relates that fact to the American's general economic understanding, and points out:

Nowhere else in the world at any time, were it a year of war, or of famine, or disaster, has any other people recorded so many bank failures in a similar period as we did. We were not experiencing a war, or a famine, or any other natural disaster. All the economic tribulations we have undergone in the past three years have been man-made troubles.

As fitting comment on Mr. Vanderlip's generalization about "economic illiteracy" appears a long article in a popular magazine by Senator Hollis, which concludes thus:

We should refuse any further reduction in the amount of their [the Allies] indebtedness, or any acceptance of German obligations as partial payments. An asset of ten to twenty billions, frozen though it be in the present depression, should be kept alive. We need not be ashamed to press a claim of this magnitude against the Powers of the world even at the risk of violating the canons of diplomacy. . . . Let us lock the notes away in our national chest, where the principal will remain intact, and the interest run on. Thus may we sit tight, and leave worry to our friends in Europe, awaiting the day when the turning tide may afford a chance to trade in the balance to our lasting good.

From the first line to the last of this article there is not one word touching the transfer difficulty, and the part which the American tariff plays therein; not the slightest hint that the one condition of payment must be an increased import by America of European goods, and that that one indispensable condition America declines to accept. All the Conferences, all the debates, all the manifestos by economists, all the books, all the reports of the last ten years, have gone for nothing so far as clarifying the one point which is most material is concerned. The Senator admits that the bankers and experts want cancellation, insist that the retention of the claims does infinite damage to finance and trade. But the bankers overlook, says the Senator, the difficulties "of the unemotional gentlemen who hold down seats in Congress," and states the Congressman's view thus:

Didn't we raise that money by giving till it hurt? Wouldn't they have lost the war if it hadn't been for our loans? That's what they said. And they promised to pay. If they don't, we've got to sweat it out of our people in taxes—in hard times, too. Just look at our deficit. A few hundred millions would come in mighty handy just now. To postpone payment on war debts, even for a twelvemonth, was a crime against the American taxpayer.

Senator Hollis says the vast majority of Americans share the view of Congress, and adds:

Since it lies within the field of their experience that individuals who fail to meet their obligations must face the courts and the sheriff, they are moved to inquire with some impatience why the Great Powers are entitled to cancellation, or even to postponement. They demand further whether there has been anything in the inception or in the handling of these war debts which exempts them from the established rule. These inquiries are logical and relevant.

And so the Senator supports the Congressman. The date of the article from which I quote is November 5, 1932, and we may take it as indicating what fourteen years of discussion have taught the public (for it would be ridiculous to claim that the European public in respect of similar problems relating to, say, Reparations has a much better standard of general understanding) of the essentials of economic education.

Nine years since this present writer delivered himself thus:

The most powerful section of our Press has consistently done its best to keep from its readers the one fact which in the interests of European peace it was necessary to impress upon them. Many aspects of the economic problem in Europe are obscure and difficult. This crucial point is clear and simple. We want Germany to pay a certain large sum; she can only do so by greatly expanding her foreign trade.

Here is a simple truth, the more general realization of which might accelerate enormously the appeasement of Europe and the solution of our own pressing economic problem. It is a national interest that it should be known. Not only have some of our largest papers not brought out its truth, they have persistently hidden it, and not only persistently hidden it, but they have insistently implied the exact contrary. Any day you may read stories of the way in which "money that ought to go to the Allies" is being spent upon public improvements, theatres, country excursions. "Why don't the Allies tax German amusements?"

It is a "little too thick" to assume that after years of discussion, of Bankers' Reports, expert explanation, the correspondents who send this kind of thing, the editors who print it, do not know that it has no bearing on the question of what Germany can pay; do not know that the printing of it merely helps to keep alive a confusion of mind that paralyses the action of statesmen and prolongs a situation fatal to the nation's most elementary interests.

But the trouble is not merely with the popular Press. Economists have tended (like other professors) to make the simple thing difficult rather than to make the difficult thing simple. When this present writer, more than twenty years ago, ventured to point out that, given the vast sums involved in modern war, a victor would be confronted with just those difficulties in recovering its cost from the vanquished outlined above, nearly all the professional economists treated the idea with contemptuous derision. Yet, again, the proposition was simple enough, was based on commonplace facts which did not demand special technical knowledge for their interpretation, and has been amply verified by the event.

It would distort altogether the case I am trying to explain if I were to leave the impression that the policies which have brought these devastations upon us were due to the influence of the "uneducated populace." The alignment is not that of the classes who have gone through our universities on the one side and those who have had no better chance than that of the National Schools on the other. The division is as between a few specialists

—economists, bankers brought into direct contact with problems of international finance,
currency experts—on the one side and the whole
public on the other. The average business man,
in America to-day, in Europe just after the war,
in his demand for "money, not goods" reveals an
economic ignorance as great as that of any coal-
heaver or charwoman. Indeed, we have mourn-
fully to recall the fact that the Imperial Finance
Committee, which put forward the figure of
twenty-four thousand millions sterling as the sum
Germany might pay, included a very eminent
banker indeed.

The educated classes, like those which formed
the governing order in Germany, were just as
subject to the follies which have nearly destroyed
us as the "uneducated" sections of the nations.
Unfortunately one must go further than that.
Education, the influence that is of academic
institutions, of the classes those institutions turned
out, of the special traditions like Nationalism
which they nurtured and developed, the philo-
sophies of life and politics most favoured by
school and university—organized education in
this sense has worsened the follies and errors
from which we have suffered. Not only, therefore,
is it true to say that most of those follies would
have been avoided if those who suffered by them
had applied the knowledge which is a commonplace of our daily lives, but it is also true to say
that education helped to obscure the commonplaces which might have saved us, and that the

errors themselves were in large part due to the express efforts of the educated classes, were in a special sense their creation.

We on the Allied side of the fence admit this readily enough when we recall the rôle played by the University in Germany in the generation which immediately preceded the war. The semi-mystic militarism, the altogether mystic Nationalism, these doctrines of the Germanic super-man, of the God-state, of Germany's mission to redeem the world, of the purifying and regenerating effect of war, were all buttressed and nursed in the universities and by the Professors of the most learned nation in the world. Dangerous nearly everywhere in this Europe of so many warring and disintegrating nationalisms, we felt the thing had reached the point of becoming a religion in Germany—although Nietzsche, Treitschke and Bernhardi were not its trinity or high priests as our war-time journalism would have us believe.

But the post-war developments in Europe have taught us—though it was evident enough before the war—that the danger is not special to Germany. One may well ask indeed whether the nationalism of the Kaiser was not amiable and anodyne compared to the potency of the Hitler or Mussolini brand, or, for that matter, of the Poincaré, and ask whether Nationalism has not become since the war an even more disruptive and explosive force than it was before.

Furthermore, on the economic side, what we

have been seeing is the destruction of Capitalism by the Capitalists—largely because they thought as Nationalists, not as Capitalists, and were unaware of the fact.

We have seen the whole of belligerent Europe pass through very grave economic revolutions. It is not merely or even mainly Russia that has suffered. We have seen the greatest commercial empire of the modern world, Britain, so disorganized and shaken as suddenly, within a decade, that is, give place in financial, industrial and commercial leadership to another; passing through an economic crisis so profound that we now begin to question whether Britain's present population can continue to live on its soil. We have seen the great middle orders—the professional classes, dependent in a special sense upon security of small savings—of Germany and Austria deprived of very nearly everything which they possessed. But these miseries just recited, the commercial and financial chaos, the collapse of money with the consequent disappearance of old people's savings and so forth—these things were not anywhere in Western Europe, either in Britain, France, Germany, Austria, Italy, the work of revolutions from below; such manifestations as the inflation in Germany were not the result of Socialist policy. They were the inevitable outcome of the policies pursued by extremely conservative governments, the result, that is, of pre-war courses which the most conservative of all the parties, together with Tory diplomats, royal houses, military chiefs, had done their best to promote.

It is not Socialism which has half ruined Western Europe and piled these troubles upon us; it is Nationalism. It is not the pacifists and internationalists who were responsible for the course which ended in utter collapse for the security of great military States; it was the "patriotic" parties.

Even where revolutionary Socialists have actually been able to capture power, as in Russia, the conditions which enabled them to do so were not the creation of Socialist agitation, the work of Socialist "plotters." The conditions which made the revolution were conditions made by war; not by Lenin, but by men of the type of Isvolsky.

One may indeed predict now of modern warfare on the world-wide scale, that it will inevitably on the side of the defeated produce revolution, and on the side of the victors (if their belligerency has been at all prolonged), the absorption and confiscation of savings and any form of property which the method of confiscation known as inflation can reach—forms, that is, like bonds, which the bourgeois and professional order are most likely to possess. One can say, further, that the organization for war must involve an increasingly complete nationalization of wealth—its mobilization under a rigid military Socialism or Communism for the purposes of war. And, finally, that prolonged world-wide war must involve everywhere profound social upheavals and, as a sequel, a greater or less degree of social—and moral—disintegration.

Capital and business, the professional and middle classes generally, having been through the experience just recently in Europe, would naturally, one would suppose, desire to eradicate the tendencies and forces which have produced such economic and social disasters, and should be anxious to repress the agitations and the agitators who tend by their influence to keep alive those destructive tendencies.

But although the breakdown of the present order has come far more from the nationalist and militarist agitator than from the Socialist, the business or professional man of Europe seems not at all anxious to repress or discourage the agitators whose doctrines actually have, by their translation into public policy, made it all but impossible for him to live in countries like Britain, dependent as such a country is on an economic internationalism which in the interests of militant nationalism has been torn to pieces. He seems very nearly as friendly as ever to those nationalist doctrines whose outcome has deprived him of his property, often destroyed his home, killed his children, and so shaken his social order generally that it is extremely doubtful whether Western civilization can now survive. The revolutionaries who actually have brought about that upheaval and are now busy planning for the next one, reviving the doctrines and policies which produced the last, are regarded by the average business man with the completest complacency. He looks with an entirely favourable eye upon such agitations. And not only that. He often— and this is true of America, too[1]—reserves his hostility for those who attempt to prevent a repetition of the revolutions and civil wars which began in 1914. He admits that that vast upheaval was the natural result of the anarchist basis of international life, of the fact that nations live with one another in "a state of nature," each a law unto himself with no organized society to give order and system to their relations; but any attempt to remedy that anarchy immediately excites his deepest hostility. Any attempt to reform it as a step to the prevention of interna-

[1] An American spectator of European conditions bears witness to the fact here dealt with. *The New Republic* (June 4, 1924) says: "It is a curious fact that the most conservative political parties are never safe guardians of the interests of property. In Germany and in France the extreme Right stands to-day, as it has stood ever since the war, for policies that make for the decay of private property. They are against the Dawes plan, against trade with Russia, against a sound fiscal policy. In England it is the 'Socialist' Government which is pushing the interests of British trade. The extreme Tories look coldly upon MacDonald's efforts to compose the Franco-German quarrel and to extend the market for British products in Russia. Our own extreme Right, led by Mr. Hughes, not only opposes American recognition of Russia, but frowns upon British and French moves in that direction, being quite unaware of the fact that the success of the Dawes plan is premised on the opening of new markets for the increased volume of industrial exports. With the best of will towards property interests the extreme Right gets squarely in their way. Its defect is one of intelligence stunted and distorted by too rigid an armour of abstract principles. The moderate radicals do not love property interests so devotedly, but their intelligence is usable. That is why property interests find it advantageous in the long run to come to terms with them."

tional disorder and its resultant ruins is met with contemptuous epithets—"pacifist," "internationalist," "socialist," just as an attempt, after the Armistice, as Mr. Churchill pointed out in the quotations I made a few moments ago, to remind "the practical business man" of the absurdities of what we were demanding merely exposed the critic to charges of pro-Germanism.

Look at certain factors of British public opinion to-day as they reflect upon the influence of the "educated" and wealthy classes. The two largest groups of our daily papers are owned by very wealthy men having very extended financial interests. For years they both opposed settlement with Germany on any practical basis; one group was especially bitter in violently attacking anyone who at that time favoured the policy to which finally in the end we had to come. I have given ample evidence on that point. The need of the policy finally adopted is not in question; there is no difference of opinion on that point at all. It is now universally agreed in England that in order to restore prosperity, in order to serve, that is, the interests of capital and finance, as well as of that of the people as a whole, we must get this Reparations and Debts confusion out of the way. Then why did three-quarters of the London Press, owned by wealthy men having immense financial interests, oppose for years what they now support?

The Communist and Socialist usually allege

that this attitude is explained by the fact that "Capitalists" have a real, not a mistakenly conceived, interest in prolonging the confusion. But this is nonsense. The confusion has nearly destroyed Capitalism. The truth, of course, is that Capitalists are very fallible and sometimes very stupid beings, just as likely as anyone else, when their education does not bear upon the facts with which they have to deal, to see those facts askew, and because they don't understand them to get excessively angry about them. Passion of retaliation, the intense desire to hit back, obscured for them, as for the rest of the population, their better judgment. And that, of course, was complicated by the fact that it is to their immediate interest as newspaper proprietors to pander to public folly by printing what the public likes to read, though so to do may be disastrous to their more remote interests as Capitalists.

At present these papers are busy rampaging against the League of Nations, deriding it, sneering at it, dwelling week after week upon its cost—which, in fact, bears precisely the same relation to our national income that the expenditure of half a crown a year would to a man having an income of £300. They propose no substitute for the League, nor present any reasoned argument against the probability that if we drift back to isolationism and international anarchy, those conditions will produce in the future what they have always produced in the past. They do not want war, they just don't want the old ways changed, or the trouble of making any organized effort to avoid political situations which produce wars, although they admit that war is so ancient and deep-rooted an institution that nothing but great changes in our way of international life can deal with it.

And so we come to a situation in which, while everybody genuinely hates war, everybody pursues policies which in the end must mean war, because they do not see the relation between the policy and its result; just as no one wanted to paralyse European resettlement or prevent the return of prosperity by insisting upon mutually exclusive demands in the matter of Reparations —or now of Debts. But our understanding of society is so defective that we simply don't see that our demands *are* mutually exclusive and must prolong the chaos. Yet this detail at least is a simple thing, and I believe within the capacity of the ordinary mind, if that mind had been developed with a clear eye to its social task. In any case, if it cannot grasp the relatively simple problems involved in avoiding these causes of dislocation, it will certainly be incapable of dealing with the immeasurably more difficult and complex problem of curing the disease which the dislocations set up.

I have taken this case of the Reparations and Debts mainly as an example, a test intended to show the degree of understanding in the public mind, as we know it, of those matters with which it has to deal. This problem of Reparations and Debts, the fact that these great sums must be paid in goods and services, if at all, is in essence extremely simple. Yet our modern publics, as voters, have to deal with problems that are not at all simple. Upon them is thrown judgment, for instance, about tariffs, one of the points chosen by Sir William Beveridge in his enumeration of the things which must be done if we are to get recovery. Professors of economics have devoted a lifetime to making the case for free trade clear, and then they have not made it very clear. But our public has to decide not merely as between straight free trade and straight protection, but a special brand of free trade, and a special brand of protection: Empire free trade. To have an opinion worth two straws about that, one would have to go at considerable length into such questions as the extent of the foreign trade, which we threaten by giving preference to Dominion trade; the possibilities in the development of Dominion trade; what prospects there are of ultimately arriving at a free-trade empire, which means some study of the politics of our chief Dominions throughout the world; how far preferences are likely to be offset by Exchange restrictions, such as those which Canada has recently imposed; what, indeed, is the relation between this problem of tariffs and the gold standard—which brings us to another trifling problem which the public will ultimately have to decide, monetary policy. Should we go back to gold? And if so, should it be at the old ratio or a new one; and if a new one, which? And all this is intimately related, of course, to the problem of international organization. Can a nation like our own afford to try the experiment of a purely national monetary standard, afford, that is, to face instability of exchange rates, instability of the value of its own money in terms of foreign currencies? We then come to the question whether it is possible to organize an international standard without international agreements touching such things as armaments, revision of treaties, pooled security, and much else.

What, in fact, is our present method of getting a decision upon these matters? In many of these things the experts disagree. The Governor of the Bank of England tells us, in effect, that he does not know what we ought to do in order to emerge from the chaos. And so we put the decision in these matters, so vital to the smooth working of our civilization, decisions upon tariffs, Empire preference, monetary standards, our place in world organization, to the judgment of the harried professional man, just running off to his surgery and popping into the polling-booth to decide what he will do about it; to the artisan at the end of his day in all the fatigue of the factory; the hazy country squire, whose dominant notion is that "these foreigners are a crafty lot"; to the charwoman, the chorus girl. . . .

The truth is, we do not face this problem. We do not face our degree of impotence and failure in meeting it. It has come upon us suddenly because invention and mechanical development have complicated the apparatus of modern life so rapidly that our political methods and our educational values have not been able to keep pace.

Now I have no panacea, but I am going to suggest that along certain lines we might so avoid certain major dislocations as to enable the machinery of civilized life to be kept running with sufficient smoothness to permit changes to be made by trial and error without bringing about collapse, sheer breakdown. I am suggesting that it is entirely within the capacity of the ordinary mind to see the disastrous nature of the policies which produce these dislocations, and that the task of enabling it to do so is the most urgent, the most feasible, and the most fundamental in the sense of being indispensable to any subsequent progress. If we are ever to achieve a conscious control and direction of all the elaborate processes of production, distribution, exchange, by which life in the modern world is maintained, we must not prepare for that by persistence in policies which make any method, any system, any rule of the road impossible. If the impulses which prompt many of our present policies are to persist, we should inevitably bring any system, Communist, Socialist, Fascist, Capitalist, technocratic, to chaos, even if we could imagine it being got smoothly under way at all.

I can make the line of my suggestion clear

most easily, perhaps, by a certain illustration or analogy which, during these lectures, I shall work rather hard—overwork, some of you may think.

When it is urged that the layman, in the matter of economic and social policy, is helpless, largely because the experts themselves are in such disagreement; when it is urged that economic science can do nothing for us, since economists themselves disagree, it is worth while to consider this point:

The doctors disagree in medicine just as much as they disagree in economics. Has the layman, therefore, been unable to derive any benefit from medical science? In answering that question I want you to give full consideration to a certain contrast; this contrast:

Much of the East—China, India, as well as most of Africa—is still ravaged by pestilences, plagues, cholera, leprosy, ophthalmia, which used to ravage our countries too, but which medical science has enabled us to abolish. That abolition has been a very great achievement. It has marked a change so great as to have had vital social and political consequences—not all of them good. That great achievement has been made possible only by the co-operation of the lay public, ignorant of medical science. Those pestilences have disappeared in the West, and still ravage the East, because the lay public in the West has proved itself capable of understanding just one or two simple points which are obscured in the mind of the lay public in the East.

To be specific: The medical expert in the West has said, "We cannot cure cholera or bubonic plague, but we can prevent those things, because with all our differences, we are at least agreed on this: that those diseases are transmitted by certain micro-organisms. If you prevent the transmission of the organism, you prevent the transmission of the disease. Keep sewage out of your drinking water, infected vermin from your homes. There is no other way of dealing with those diseases, because it is quite impossible to cure them by things out of a bottle, or, indeed, to handle them at all, once they have got a grip in an epidemic."

When the medical experts have thus talked to the lay public in the West, that public has grasped the point; has, through appropriate sanitary authorities, taken, in the way indicated, the necessary steps to prevent transmission of disease. It has been willing so to take the trouble— sometimes the measures have been extensive and complicated, involving much expenditure, inspection, and the rest of it—because the layman saw the essential point.

But why did he see a point with which the man of the Eastern community either did not see or did not trouble about? The layman in China or in India, the mass of people, are in very many respects as intelligent as our people in the West. There is certainly no *inherent* superiority of intelligence on the part of the Westerner, as some of the great successes among Hindu scientists abundantly prove. You may retort that the reason for the relative failure of sanitary measures in the East is the looseness of the social organization. Yet in much of the East you have more complete power on the part of government, less democracy, than in the West. Moreover, in some respects, Eastern society, Hindu society particularly, is very highly organized by methods that seem to have had originally a sanitary motive. I refer, of course, to certain features of the caste system, with its ritual cleansing, avoidance of contamination, and so forth.

Why, in the last analysis, then, has prophylaxis so far succeeded in the West as to have wiped out these diseases, and to have encountered in the East obstacles in the lay public which still prevent any corresponding measure of success? Why, in other words, have we of the West managed to rid ourselves of bubonic plague, cholera, leprosy, while the East has not? I suggest that the layman of the West has been able to make use of the medical but not of the economic experts, because we bring to medical things, to physical phenomena, a scientific attitude, an intellectual discipline which we do not bring to the study of social, economic and political phenomena. To these problems we bring much the same type and temper of mind which the East still brings even to physical phenomena like the causation of diseases. We used to have that type and temper of mind ourselves in dealing with physical phenomena; but we have replaced it by what we call the scientific attitude. When the medical expert tells a Chinese or an Indian community that, in order to prevent the spread of a pestilence, it must kill rats, exterminate vermin, keep drinking-water clean, adopt certain methods in the disposal of sewage, he encounters, not an inherent incapacity on the part of very quick-witted Indians or Chinese to understand that process of disease transmission which prompts the expert's recommendation; but the expert encounters a whole habit of mind and life which is rebellious to taking the necessary measures. First an innate fatalism. The Oriental is apt to argue that "you get the pestilence or you don't. Some escape. Some do not. Who is to tell why? Plainly it is fate." Or, if the explanation has a more religious tinge, it is the anger of gods, the presence of devils wreaking vengeance. In any case, such measures as those recommended by the fussy busybodies of the West disturb established and settled habits of a conservative community. The measures are not only, it is felt, an interference with the course of nature, an attempt to rebel against fate or the will of God, but an insufferable nuisance, and fatal to a quiet life. Far better to take such chances as life affords. And, of course, the injunctions about the destruction of rats and other vermin may encounter deep religious conviction or prejudice. In other words, the policy encounters the obstinate resistance of a whole habit of thought and a confirmed outlook.

Much of that attitude was ours in Europe only a few generations ago. Every measure of prophylaxis has had to meet the resistance, not, it is true, to the same degree, but the same kind of resistance it has still to encounter in the East. In dealing, however, with physical phenomena, it has largely disappeared, and we have replaced it by a philosophy of cause and effect, applying inductive methods of reasoning, doubt, examination. We bring to plainly physical problems the detached, scientific mind. We know what we want in such matters. In dealing with inventions, industrial processes, we know that we want to achieve certain quite definite ends, to create certain things, to get them moved from one place to another for instance. We have clearly the aim before us, and the means are not usually diverted or neutralized by other, contradictory aims in our own minds. But I suggest that we have not yet learned the trick of approaching political, economic and social phenomena in the same spirit.

Note this: our success in this matter of the pestilences—where the Easterner fails—is not due to the fact that we have included bacteriology in the school curriculum. It is not in the least necessary so to do. Given a certain habit or way of thought, the facts of the matter so readily become apparent and convincing that we don't need to "learn the subject" at all. And I do not believe that the way to improve general understanding of public policy is to introduce new subjects into the curriculum like Economics or Civics, by media of text-books packed with facts and information. The trouble is not lack of "information." The trouble is that we don't use the information we already possess. The facts which would have enabled us to see the folly of the course we took over Reparations and Debts are self-evident facts, supplied by the internal evidence of the situation. It is obvious that if no goods —things to eat, wear, use—are added to a nation's store, no wealth is added to its store; that "money" is only wealth at the point where it can be exchanged for those things. A savage, a primitive Esquimaux or Zulu, would see the point immediately because his mind is not bemused by the money illusion.

The intellectual problem involved in understanding the point about Debts and Reparations is not one whit more complicated or difficult than the intellectual problem involved in understanding the microbic theory of disease. In one sense, indeed, the economic problem is very much easier, because the evidence which reveals it is the internal evidence or facts of common knowledge; whereas much of the microbic theory of disease is founded upon highly technical investigations, upon facts which could not be revealed at all except by means of long technical investigations.

I suggest, therefore, that our first task is to find out what prevents our understanding such fundamentally simple things; to find out why we succeed with relative ease in the matter of the microbes and fail so disastrously in the matter of money.

I suggest, further—as a hint of what will follow—that we go astray on such things as Debts and Reparations, not merely because our conceptions of money are crudely distorted, but because our conceptions touching even simpler things have become distorted. I think we shall discover, for instance, that we have harboured ideas as to what a nation is that are crudely and self-evidently false; that we have not really asked ourselves what we want of governments and politics; have not even decided whether we even *want* to find the way of escape. And until we are sure that we want it, we certainly shall not find it.

If it should prove true that all this time we have not really been wanting prosperity, but quite other things, then that may give a very useful hint as to why we do not avoid the economic pestilence as easily as we do the physical one.

II

THE DISBELIEF IN ECONOMIC
SANITATION

LET me remind you of sufficient of my text to make it clear what I am trying to show:
My propositions are:—

(1) That much of our present chaos could have been avoided if the big publics which make and unmake governments had avoided courses which practically all the experts agree inevitably cause disastrous dislocation, ill health in the economic organism; and that if the size and difficulty of the problem had been thus reduced the public would have had a better chance of seeing the right course in what remained of the difficulty.

(2) That the rationale of these causes of economic dislocation and ill health are not inherently more difficult to see than that microbic theory of disease, which the very inexact science of medicine has managed to make understandable to the lay public, and so to do that public very great service.

(3) That the reason why the public do not see the economic truth as they do see the

medical truth is that we apply to the understanding of physical phenomena, matter, a scientific method and spirit which we abandon when we judge economic—which is also largely political and social—phenomena.

Our problem is to discover why this difference of approach.

I take it, of course, as a common assumption that the maintenance of health in the social organism, the avoidance of pestilence, is indispensable to successful changes of regimen, to necessary transformations, to the conscious control or direction, to desired ends. Although we may disagree as to the nature of the surgical operation which a patient's condition calls for, we can agree that it is undesirable that he should be suffering from typhus or cholera when we operate, whether on brain, limb or abdomen. Or, to make the analogy more mechanical, it is easier to modify a defective system working with relative smoothness than to bring a good system out of utter chaos. Our society resembles an aeroplane: if the machine stops it crashes, with infinite misery as a result. If alterations are necessary, they must be made while the machine is running.

And let me remind you quite briefly of the facts to which I appealed.

For considerably over ten years in Europe we have seen this situation; all the economists, all the bankers, all the serious students of public affairs, persistently urging one line of economic policy; i.e. (ruthlessly to scale down or wipe out Reparations and Debts, *or* so reduce tariffs as to increase the creditors' imports); and all the governments, supported by nearly all the politicians, persistently taking exactly the contrary line. And this refusal of the governments to do what every expert has declared must be done if prosperity is to be re-established has ended by reducing the world to economic chaos, by making the economic confusion which the war produced already bad enough, worse confounded. The most recent illustration is the line taken by politicians and public in America over the Debts—a line directly contrary to that urged by American economists and experts.

Governments have thus, against the direct counsel of all their expert advisers, persisted in a line of policy which has worsened the depression, prolonged the chaos, broadly because if they had not thus consented to follow the wrong policy, and had insisted upon following the right, they would have been torn from power by angry electorates who were sure that they knew better than the financial experts in financial matters, better than the economists in economics; just as in China and in India Western doctors have been unable to abolish cholera, plague and typhus because the recommendations to keep sewage out of drinking-water and vermin from houses and persons are either disregarded because of an innately fatalistic habit of mind ("disease is inevitable; you get the plague or you don't, whatever you do about it") or because the population of those countries are sure they know more of the causation of disease than the Western medicine man; that cholera and plague and other diseases are sent by angry devils who must be scared away by banging drums or other ancient and well-known traditional methods.

Our electorates are at the stage of understanding in economic matters that the Easterners are in the matter of sanitation and its relation to disease.

Touching this medical analogy, by the way, a medical member of the audience at my last lecture has sent me some interesting reflections.

He says:

I'm wondering if the analogy couldn't be carried further.

The methods adopted in matters medical might go much further—if the public would let them. The "educated" and wealthy members of this public would still rather pay a man £100 for the spectacular result of the removal of an appendix, though they'd consider £5 a big fee to any medico who gave them such advice as would render the removal of the appendix most unlikely ever to be necessary.

In these days we as "specialists" see that we approach medicine from the wrong end—not because we want to but because our public still insist on *treatment* of disease by something in a bottle rather than the prevention of disease by a rational—and necessary—mode of living.

Medical treatment—as the public still insists on having it—is only necessary because preventive or prophylactic medicine has failed. Surgical treatment is only necessary because *both* prophylaxis and treatment on the medical side have failed, and yet

The Surgeon gets 100 guineas.

The Physician gets 3 guineas.

The advisor in Prophylaxis probably gets nothing.

Just as the successful General gets a peerage and £100,000.

The Statesmen get what is equivalent to the Physician's fee.

The Pacifist who gives his life to trying to make the General's work unnecessary gets nothing but kicks.

Even the Anaesthetist, who has often a more responsible and trying job than the Surgeon, gets a twentieth or less of the Surgeon's fee—the job being of course so much less spectacular.

A well-known Surgeon said to me yesterday: "I'm afraid we shall never educate the public into being ready to pay a surgeon £100 for operating and £200 for deciding that an operation isn't necessary. It needs only practice and manual dexterity to do most operations, it needs much *more* thought, knowledge, experience and courage to decide against operation.

On the other hand in the conduct of their jobs when not in any way dependent on a public opinion, they have progressed as the knowledge of economics has progressed, that is, they approach their surgical *procedure* now at the right end.

In pre-Lister days most surgical wounds went septic. Then methods were discovered to counteract the poison germs that got into the surgical wounds, i.e. TREATING *the disease*. Now, of course, it is absolutely a prophylactic technique and Surgeons *prevent* any germs getting into wounds.

Surgery is in its conduct aseptic.

Medicine is still only *anti*septic. There is great hope, however. It is one of the compensations in the widespread Panel practice. It pays the Doctor with a large Panel to educate his patients in the way of preventing disease.

The next stage of my argument leads us immediately into the relation of human nature to economic and political problems, a relationship which cannot in practice be ignored.

Whenever it is pointed out that the essential

issue of, say, the Reparations problem is an extremely simple one, and that really an education which professed to equip students for under-standing the nature of the world in which they will have to live—whenever that is pointed out, the reply is generally that the mass fail to see the point, not because they are inadequately equipped educationally, but because anger and bitterness blind them to simple facts. We were determined to punish Germany, our moral indignation made us so anxious for retribution, that we could not consider the facts at all.

Well, I suggest that we should be nearer the truth if we turned the explanation the other way about; instead of saying that we did not see the facts because we were angry, it would be truer to say that we were angry because we did not see the facts. We did not see them because we had fallen unconsciously, or been pushed by certain features of our education, into utterly false inter-pretations of certain simple phenomena of the external world. When I say that we did not see the facts, I do not refer for the moment to the facts about Reparations, I mean the facts as to what a nation is. We were passionate in our hatred of Germany, because we saw Germany as a "per-son." But there is no such "person." That is an abstraction we have built up by the use of symbols, a way of speech. The use of certain words has led to a way of thought; led us to see facts in a certain way, a fantastic way. But for this distor-tion we should not have had these angers, or not had them to the degree which prevented our seeing such simple truths as that Germany could only pay in goods.

I can perhaps clarify the point I am trying to make as to the relation of our perception of external fact to the direction taken by our emotions by a parable or an analogy:

I have nursed for many years a deadly hatred of an enemy, and have sworn to kill him if I should encounter him. Suddenly, one day, I see him across the street. A friend, who is with me, and who knows my story and my oath, argues with me, and begs me to restrain my passion. But my hate smothers reason and I take my pistol, bent upon murder. Here, indeed, is one of those cases where reason is so feeble and emotion is so powerful that one would say the former has no chance as a guide of conduct. And yet it is reason, pure logic, which finally turns me from my course and diverts completely the direction of my emotions. As the man across the street, seeing my pistol, raises his hands I see that both have five fingers. My enemy had a finger missing on his right hand. Because my mind, even then, goes through a certain logical process which enables me to interpret facts in a certain way, my passion falls from me. I see that it is a case of mistaken identity.

This profound change of behaviour is not accounted for by any change in my nature, by a long discipline of suppressing emotions. Nothing of the sort. I saw facts in a certain way, and no effort of repression or change of nature was necessary. But it is possible that if the logical processes of my mind had been obscured by theories of witchcraft or superstition, if I had been taught to believe that an evil man could grow fingers as he needs them—the sort of belief that was common enough in Europe in the Middle Ages, and is common enough in Africa to-day —I should not have interpreted external fact in just the way that I did. But note again that this different interpretation would have been due to a difference of education.

Let us see the application of this parable.

When, during the war, on the morrow of some outrageous barbarity like the sinking of the *Lusitania*, I would get the question: "Don't you loathe Germans?" I would reply: "Don't you loathe the people living along the London and North Eastern Railway? A season ticket holder has just been found guilty of an outrage upon a little girl." The retort, of course, would be that people living along the line of the London and North Eastern Railway don't make an entity— a "moral unit" that can be held responsible— any one member of which can be held responsible for the behaviour of the rest. But do the people of Germany whom we were fighting, remember, largely because we had declared their government to be an autocracy over whose actions the people had little control, a people made up of most diverse elements, Socialists and Junkers, Jews and Catholics—do all these make a single unit that we can hate or love?

On my recent visit to the U.S.A. the head of the history department of a great university, during a discussion of the Debt problem, put this question to me: "Is Europe sincere? Has she not really been planning to welsh on her debts and to throw dust in America's eyes, and does she not intend, a few years hence, to unite against America?" And I wondered by what process a man learned in the events of history, deeply erudite, could at the end think of Europe as an entity having definable "intentions," a single personality that could be "sincere" or "insincere." I am afraid that a few years earlier he would have asked me about the villainy of Germany and the grandeur of France. He would have distinguished very sharply between Germans and French. (America was particularly subject to this sort of mania.) He was now ready to lump them all together, and make of them one corporate body, one mind. This was not because there had been any real change in national character, but because it is not a real thing at all of which he spoke: it is a symbol, a fantasy, a shadow, created by a way of thought. How completely and fantastically this is true in such cases was proven to me when, as a boy, circumstances carried me on to a remote part of the American frontier. An election was toward; politicians, in the true Big Bill Thompson style, were perpetually bringing George III into their harangues. And nothing was more popular, was such good politics. Audiences howled with pleasurable hate when some demagogue would enlarge upon the detestable qualities of "the English." Most of the audience, of course, had never seen an Englishman. When they responded so readily it was not because of any quality, good, bad, or indifferent in Englishmen. It was the picture they made in their minds, or had made for them, which caused their hate. They saw a certain fact of the world about them—the existence of forty million people on an island in the other hemisphere—in a certain way; they saw it as a tyrannical "person" threatening their freedom and welfare, ready to enslave them and destroy their homes. There is, of course, no such "person." But to them he was a real person, with definite features and qualities, arrogant, avaricious, with a long drooping moustache, a monocle, and talking with an absurd drawl. They had never seen such a person; never would see him, and to the English boy who had come amongst them and to certain English men and women who were to follow, they were for the most part exceedingly kind, and of them entertained no such feeling. As an American once said to me, he hated the Englishman "in the abstract" only. But the Englishman does not exist in the abstract; he only exists in the concrete. From the moment that we so read facts as to see that the thing we hate is a shadow, a figment of our minds, our feelings take different directions. A savage is terror-struck at his own reflection in a glass; but his fears evaporate when he learns the nature of a mirror: the same external fact interpreted by his mind in one way creates one emotion; the same external fact read in another produces an entirely different emotion or none.

Preposterous conceptions touching the nature of nations have grown up in our minds, because at some point we have allowed ourselves to part company with plain fact. We commonly speak of nations as "she." Pictorial representation of nations in political cartoons and so on are always as persons: John, or Jonathan or Marianne. It is a simple nursery method. But we don't observe, probably, that in our minds these pictures are no longer symbols; that they have become actual persons; biological organisms with a single will and responsibility. We have parted company with external reality as much as the inmate who insists that he is made of glass and will crack if you shake his hand.

"They drowned my brother," said an Allied airman, when asked his feelings on a reprisal bombing raid over German cities. Thus, because an officer from Hamburg, himself under orders, is responsible for drowning an Englishman in the North Sea, an old woman in a garret in Freiburg, or some children, who have but dimly heard of the war, and could not even remotely be held responsible for it, or have pre-vented it, are killed with a clear conscience because they are German. We cannot understand the Chinese, who punish one member of a family for another's fault; yet that is very much more rational than the conception which we accept as the most natural thing in the world. It is never questioned, indeed, until it is applied to ourselves. When the acts of British troops in Ireland or India, having an extraordinary resemblance to German acts in Belgium, are taken by certain American newspapers as showing that "Britain" (i.e. British people) is a bloodthirsty monster who delights in the killing of unarmed priests or peasants, we know that somehow the foreign critic has got it all wrong. We then immediately realize that for some Irishman or Indian to dismember a charwoman or decapitate a little girl in Somersetshire, because of the crime of some Black and Tan in Cork, or English general at Amritsar, would be unadulterated savagery, a sort of dementia. In any case the poor folk in Somerset were not responsible; millions of English folk are not. They are only dimly aware of what goes on in India or Ireland, and are not really able in all matters, by any means, to control their government—any more than the Americans are able to control theirs.

Yet the idea of responsibility attaching to a whole group, as justification for retaliation, is a very ancient idea, savage, almost animal in its origin. And anything can make a collectivity. To one small religious sect in a village it is the members of a rival sect who are the enemies of the human race; in the mind of the tortured negro in the Congo any man, woman, or child of the white world could fairly be punished for the pains that he has suffered.[1] The conception has doubtless arisen out of something protective, some instinct useful, indispensable to the race; as have so many of the instincts which, applied unadapted to altered conditions, become socially destructive.

Incidentally, note how all the machinery of Press control and war-time colleges of propaganda prepared the public mind for the extremely difficult task of the settlement and Treaty-making that lay before it. (It was a task in which everything indicated that, unless great care were taken, public judgment would be so swamped in passion that a workable peace would be impossible.) The more tribal and barbaric aspect of the conception of collective responsibility was fortified by the intensive and deliberate exploitation of atrocities during the years of the war. The atrocities were not just an incident of war-time news: the principal emotions of the struggle came to centre around them. Millions, whom the obscure political debate behind the conflict left entirely cold, were profoundly moved by these stories of cruelty and barbarity committed by a "person"—the enemy.

[1] An American playwright has indicated amusingly with what ingenuity we can create a "collectivity." One of the characters in the play applies for a chauffeur's job. A few questions reveal the fact that he does not know anything about it. "Why do you want to be a chauffeur?" "Well, I'll tell you, boss. Last year I got knocked down by an automobile and badly hurt. And I made up my mind that when I came out of the hospital I'd get a bit of my own back. Get even by knocking over a few guys, see?" A policy of "reprisals," in fact.

When this type of fantasy is common, there is no infamy of which kindly, humane, and emotionally moral people may not prove themselves capable; no moral contradiction or absurdity of which they may not approve. Anything may become right, anything may become wrong.

The evil is not only in its resultant inhumanities. It lies much more in the fact that this development of moral blinkers deprives us of the capacity to see where we are going, and what we are crushing underfoot; and that may well end by our walking over the precipice.

The feeling which moved us during the Treaty-making could only have arisen because we were possessed of this conception of nations as moral entities, with a single will like a biological organism, a conception which arises first from the need of symbols to express a fact, and then from treating the symbol *as* the fact. The transition is quite unconscious. This confusion between symbols and the fact they stand for is a commonplace of savage thought, is a strong tendency in most minds, and is a tendency which our education, far from warning us against, far from aiming at creating an awareness of in our minds, seems directly to encourage.

During the period of the Treaty-making we wanted to punish "Germany," and all questions of financial and economic possibility were lost in Niagaras of moral indignation.

"By what means can Germany pay these sums?" you asked. And the reply you got was that Ger-

many plotted to enslave mankind—just as to-day
when you ask an American by what means Europe
is to pay, you get the counter-question of whether
she hired the money. But I am suggesting that
we only got into that state by persisting to think
of Germany as a "person." We were told that
before Germany could be forgiven, she "must
repent"; otherwise she must be punished.

Who would be punished? The little underfed
girls and boys then trooping to school? Were
they the criminals? Or the old woman picking up
sticks in the forest? Had *she* made the war?

The public mind seems to have fallen grievously
into the same trap in its attitude towards the
League of Nations. The League, too, has come
to be for great numbers an entity quite apart
from the governments that can compose it.
Large masses are hostile to any very definite
commitment to League obligations, to any commitment, that is, by which the League could
possibly possess power to act with any decision
and authority. If you ask such a sceptic why he
refuses to allow his country to be bound by these
commitments, he will reply: "Because the League
is such a feeble, impotent thing." Having refused
to assent to the only measures which could
possibly give the League power, he criticizes the
League for having no power, and makes that a
ground for objecting to giving it any. The
bitterest criticisms of the League impotence
come from the self-same persons who always
oppose any step by the constituent States which

might give the organization some power. The contradiction of the two positions is very rarely seen, because the League, like the nation, has become in their minds an entity quite apart from its constituent elements.

This was notably the case in the Sino-Japanese crisis. When the crisis arose the British Press as a whole took the line that Britain should remain neutral; should on no account take a line which might "alienate" Japan; and then criticized the League because it did not act with more decision in restraint of Japan. Two groups of popular papers in London violently urged British dissociation from the League because it had been so impotent!

Now, is it seriously argued that it is beyond the power of education to develop the particular skill or aptitude which would enable us to notice when we had slipped from using words as symbols and had come to regard them as things? But the tendency of education, instead of doing this is to pile more facts on to those which we have already misinterpreted; to have our children "learn about foreign countries"; to add to the geography or history of Britain, already loathed, that of Germany or France; to organize visits of French or German boys or girls to our schools, or our boys to theirs, which is certainly imposing very severe strains upon human nature. Only a psychological miracle could prevent such visitors being heartily detested, although the youngsters will dutifully express the sentiments which they know are expected of them. That does not get to the root of the thing at all. For one thing we don't cease to dislike people, even though they be only the embodiment of an abstraction, because we know them: witness the bitter hatred between Catholic and Protestant in Ireland and elsewhere; between Hindoo and Mohammedan, living in the same street. That does not get to the root of the matter. The root consists of a certain way of interpreting external tact; a way of thought.

Whenever I read an article on the subject of international like and dislike, or see a heading such as "Why Europe Hates America," or "The Briton's Attitude to the United States," I have a feeling of entering a region of phantasmagoria, of dealing in entities that have no real existence, of, again, treating symbols and images as though they were living persons.

I suppose I have heard as many generalizations about the English from the French, about the French from the English, about Americans from both, and about both from Americans, as any man, for I happen to have divided my life between the three countries. And the truest thing I could say about these generalizations is that they are all and always false in lesser or greater degree. By their very nature they must be.

The best warning I have heard about such generalizations was from the lips of a little girl aged seven. Her English parents had just settled in New York and we were discussing the attitude of Americans to British, and vice versa. A little wearied of the line the talk had taken, I turned to the seven-year-old daughter of the family and asked: "How do *you* like Americans, Ethel?" Now Ethel had been placed in charge of a mammy, a negress from Alabama, of whom she had come to have a very high opinion indeed. When I asked Ethel her opinion of Americans she, with truer discrimination than her elders had been showing, put a counter-question: "Well, do you mean Black or White Americans?" She felt she could speak in some measure for the former, but was less sure of the latter.

This child realized that a nation is not a unit; that every great modern nation is composed of differing races, religions, classes, interests; that you cannot take a Scot, a Welshman, a Yorkshire-man, Catholic, Nonconformist, Communist, Peer, and then ask whether you like "it," or think "she" is a likeable person, "she" being Great Britain. As well ask whether you like people who live in odd-numbered houses as distinct from the detestable people who live in even-numbered houses.

All these generalizations start on the assump-tion of there being a number of entities, "persons" having distinct and single wills. In the ten years of my life in the United States I have heard some hundreds of expressions of opinion as to the "intentions" of Great Britain—or Germany, or just "Europe." Within a few days of writing these lines I received a long letter from a correspondent in the United States, enclosing some literature issued by a peace organization in favour of America's joining the World Court. My correspondent says:

A child could detect the hand of Britain in this propaganda. . . . The American people are admittedly rather ignorant of world politics; and much less we care. But one of the things we have made up our mind about is that we will never enter that British-made caucus called the League of Nations. . . . Britain has evidently decided that the note now to strike is piety and peace. Her intention in supporting this propaganda is now to concentrate upon the destruction of our Nationalism, and then later. . . .

And there follows a detailed programme of what "Britain" intends to do in the matter of enslaving America during the next twenty years, just as we used to indulge a few years since in dogmatic assertions about Germany's "intentions" to invade Great Britain, destroy the Empire, and subjugate the world.

Now, if you were to ask this extremely dogmatic student of "Britain's intentions" what the intentions of his own country were at the next general election, or the intentions of his own city about the next mayor, he would probably immediately confess that he did not know, and that nobody could know. I have known New Yorkers and New York newspapers on the eve of a mayoralty election give cocksure forecasts which twenty-four hours later were proved to be utterly erroneous. But though this American cannot tell you what his own city will do a week hence, he delivers himself with complete assurance on the "intentions" during the next twenty years of forty million people deeply divided in their political creeds and social outlook; a people who have introduced radically new principles into legislation, innovations which no one a quarter of a century ago would have predicted; a people into whose lives factors of deep change have been introduced, the total effect of which it is plainly impossible to foresee.

Of course, it may be true that when you take a Catholic Highlander, a Protestant Lowlander, a Wesleyan Welshman, a cockney sceptic, a Channel Island Frenchman, or as many different racial, religious, or political elements as you please, and put them within the same political boundaries, you may develop, despite their racial, religious, linguistic, social, or other differences, certain common characteristics which make them all "British"; as you can take the down-easter from the State of Maine, the New York Jew, the southern darky, and make of the lot "Americans."

But you cannot, save by a sort of mental blindness, or imagery, attach to the entity so created those qualities about which we are apt to quarrel. I sometimes hear my countrymen telling me that they find "Americans" boastful and hostile to Britains; as my American friends tell me that they find "the English" supercilious and hostile to "Americans." But one knows that there is no means of testing these generalizations by the sort of factual data that one would require in any ordinary conclusion related to practical life. There is no thermometer by which you can test whether the degree of dislike which a given white American evinces toward a given English-man, who is a foreigner, is greater than the same American feels toward a negro or Jew, who is an American.

But I suspect the generalization as a statement of fact for reasons related to that "personification" of the nation just touched upon, and which I find myself, despite my own analysis of this thing, falling into. If, in London, in the course of a week, I were treated with discourtesy by, say a bus conductor, a railway employee, a policeman, I should probably merely say to myself that I had encountered a trio of discourteous boors. If it happened at a time of, say, a general strike, I should say that the strike was beginning to affect tempers. The question of "national charac-teristics" would not enter. But if it happened in America I should probably, despite all the warn-ings of my reflections on these things, begin to generalize about "a certain uncouthness in American manners." I should do that, though it had never occurred to me to ascribe the experience to "English" manners when it happened in London.

The habit of regarding a nation as a moral unit or entity is not only a source of recrimination in so far as it causes us to attribute certain moral qualities to the "effigy" we create in our minds, but is the root of certain economic fallacies intimately related to this very problem of seeing "the way of escape" which we are discussing. We in Europe talk of the competition of "America," a portent to be feared, as we used to talk of Germany. But there is no commercial corporation doing trade known as "Germany" or "America." A coffee plantation in Brazil buys electrical machinery in Westphalia, and the factory owner or hands, with money so obtained, buy canned beef from Argentine; the Argentinian with money so obtained buys cutlery in Sheffield. Is that Brazilian, German, Argentinian, or British trade? Pennsylvanians do not talk of Pennsylvania trade as being in competition with Massachusetts trade. But we should do so if the fight of the North American colonies against the mother country had developed as the fight of the South American colonies did, and if Pennsylvania and Massachusets had been distinct nations as well as distinct States. The difference, however, if Pennsylvania and Massachusetts were nations, would be one of political status, not of economic fact. If the competition is not there without the purely political attribute of nationhood (because statehood has stopped short of nationhood), why is it there merely because certain purely political rights of independence have been added? The notion of economic rivalry results from the sense of political or national difference.

Indeed, this conception of the nation as a person, and the hostilities to which it gives rise, accounts for economic confusions far more than is generally assumed. Economists have tackled

Protectionism with somewhat elaborate economic arguments. But the cause of Protectionism is after all political—it lies in this conception of nations as economic units or entities; in the ideas which we have formed of what constitutes "us" and what the "foreigner"; in obscure political animosities more than in any calculated economic interest by a whole people. A recent experience in America in connection with the debts discussion brought this home. One of the proposals which arose about debts was to the effect that Britain might settle hers by selling Canada to the United States. Now this proposal was made at the very time that the people making it were clamouring for an increase in the tariff against Canadian imports. Those imports, they said, were bad for American trade, American prosperity. Yet if Canada were transferred to the United States, the same imports, the same goods that is, manufactured in the same factories, by the same hands, would enter what is now the United States territory without any let or hindrance at all. If commodities from Ontario are bad for trade in Michigan or Illinois when one kind of flag flies in Ontario, how, by what process, do the same commodities become good for Michigan or Illinois when a slightly different kind of flag flies in Ontario?

We assume that because a political unit—or rather a unit of political sovereignty—exists, *therefore* that must be made the economic unit. But why? The thing is a complete *non sequitur*,

F

And it threatens to make European civilization quite unworkable.

Here on one page of the morning paper you may read the latest details of the Central and South-Eastern European financial collapse; that the League Council has refused to grant further loans to Austria and Greece because loans would prove no solution, the money would be spent and the fundamental insolvency remain as great as ever. It is explained—and agreed apparently on all hands—that no financial recovery is possible so long as countries like the Danubian States continue deliberately to break up essentially inter-dependent areas by ever-increasing tariffs; that not until something resembling the freedom of economic exchange which the old Hapsburg Empire ensured is restored can those countries ever hope to regain stable prosperity. And then, after reading of those latest results of economic nationalism (the results happen to be chaos and ruin), one turns over the page to read, in the latest news from Dublin, of the view of Mr. De Valera as to the best way to grapple with the economic disasters which afflict the world. That way, he tells us, is for each country to be as self-sufficing as possible; which means that each *cultural group* is to be a self-sufficient economic unit—the cultural divisions having arisen long before the modern world of steam and power, and having usually not the faintest relationship to any natural economic division. Mr. De Valera announces the means by which he proposes to put this principle into effect for Ireland. He proposes, as a first contribution to the maladjustments from which the world suffers, that the Irish tax-payer shall be further taxed in order to permit the Irish farmer to grow more wheat (since more wheat, which the Canadian is sometimes burning, is what the world now needs apparently); and as it would be plainly immoral for Erse-speaking people to eat flour ground by non-Erse-speaking, he proposes to have the subsidized wheat ground, not in large modern mills, but in country mills. For these purposes there are to be not merely tariffs but control of import by licence. The project in its details has been worked out, appropriately enough, by a mediaevalist historian. The Irish correspondent of the *Manchester Guardian* writes:

Though a wheat-growing policy has long been in Mr. De Valera's mind, the credit for this bold scheme for saving the Free State's local mills must go to Professor Alfred O'Rahilly, of Cork. His active and ingenious mind could not be content with the academic study of Catholic principles underlying the sociology and political economy of the Middle Ages. He determined to see those principles applied to present-day conditions in the Free State. He has for years been carrying on a crusade for the salvation of the Free State flour-milling industry, and has worked out a scheme for its reorganization which is to include the revival of local wheat-growing and the fixation of the just price for the product. Undoubtedly it is the Professor's scheme which Mr. De Valera is preparing to put into execution. But the consumer is assured that the price he pays will not be permitted to exceed the world price. Presumably, when wheat is to be grown locally the gap between the world price and the just price will be filled by a subsidy, coming out of the pocket of some person or persons unknown.

And milling is, of course, only one of the industries which Mr. De Valera is determined to develop
by taxing all other industries. There must be
Irish boots, Irish shirts, Irish tools, and to-morrow
perhaps Irish ships. (Ship subsidies are the most
popular of the means by which the Nationalist
taxes Peter to subsidize Paul, and Paul to subsidize Peter.) The Irish are to live, not so much
by taking in each other's washing, as by cutting
off increasing slices of each other's shirts. This
as a prelude to "world economic recovery."

But, after all, in the midst of the most intensive
"Buy British" campaign in history, can we re-
proach the Irish for being thoroughgoing in their
"Buy Irish" campaign? We, too, have our wheat-
quota schemes, our vast subsidies to British
beets, and the rest. Like Mr. De Valera, who
thinks that if he can put a hundred Irish mill-
hands into employment by turning a hundred
English out, he is "helping to solve the unemployment problem"; so we, by subsidizing beet
extravagantly and helping to ruin the West
Indies, are quite persuaded that we are "helping
to solve agricultural depression." That the unem-
ployed English mill-hand is not going to buy
Irish bacon or butter and *is*, by his artificially
created unemployment, going to add to the unemployment in Irish dairies and bacon factories, is
a fact which does not enter into Mr. De Valera's
picture; for if it did, he would cease to think of
this as an "Irish" problem and begin to think of
it as an economic problem, a habit which would be

fatal to the philosophy of life which he embodies, and which, so long as it is common, is going to make the creation of a prosperous and workable world impossible.

The Prime Minister, not long since, had a phrase which gets to the heart of this fallacy and the significance of which—especially when taken in the particular context in which it appears— does not seem quite to have been grasped. Mr. MacDonald said:

We are now preparing for the Economic Conference which is due to meet in Ottawa at the middle of July. The great obstacle to world prosperity (after Reparations) is that of nationalism removed from its proper sphere of cultural and political liberty and made the justification for restrictions in international trade. These, when carried to the lengths to which some States have carried them, mean the impoverishment of the whole world. At Ottawa, I believe, we can lay the foundations of an economic policy which will be mutually helpful to the members of the Commonwealth, but which will not be paralysing to general world commerce. We can create freer trade conditions over a vast area of the world.

The thing is worth a little exploration, since so often Protectionism is attacked on its economic side when its essence is non-economic. If we are to remedy the dislocations to which the economic machine is liable—dislocations difficult enough to remedy in any case—we have to consider economic things, the fact that since this area is poor for agricultural possibilities, but rich in metals, it should be used for metals and developed in conjunction with that coalfield; these two things must be put together for the increase of human welfare. But the economic Nationalist does not approach the matter from that end at all. He says: The coal is foreign; the peasants now starving on that poor metalliferous soil speak Erse or Gaelic or Friese; we cannot ask them to become prosperous miners, for that would make them part of an international process, would break up the national economic unit. Moreover, the country which has the coal would not take our metals even if we mined them, for it, too, objects to foreign products. Our economic units must not be made that way. The question is not whether this area is for economic purposes complementary to that, making thus a productive unit; the question is: "Who makes part of our nation, who speaks like us, uses our oaths, and has our tastes in cookery?" In order to ensure that all trading and exchange is done between members of the national group, we shall compel our people to raise farm-stuffs on soil which ought to be given over to mines, and fuel from what ought to be farm land.

So Mr. De Valera says: "Buy Irish" as we say "Buy British"—or rather he says: "Buy Southern Irish." Until Ulster makes part of his "cultural group," goods from Ulster are to be kept out as causing unemployment. But if Ulster came into the Free State those goods would then apparently be innocuous; they would cease to be a cause of unemployment. But why? Again, they would be the same goods made by the same people. Dublin would no longer complain of the competition of Belfast and refuse its goods. But, once more, why not? If they are undesirable in one political condition, are they desirable in another—if economic welfare is what we are thinking about at all?

And Ireland is not the only nation in the British Isles. Already you may see in Scotland signs which say, "Buy Scots," and in Wales "Buy Welsh." And, again, why not? If self-sufficient units is the remedy, why not *these* cultural units? And when the Cornish tongue has been revived we shall have "Buy Cornish." Indeed, why wait for the dead tongues to come alive? Why limit the prescription of self-sufficiency to each *nation*? Why not the county? As economic divisions they are neither more nor less justifiable than the national boundaries. And why these purely geographical boundaries? Why not "Buy Angli-can," "Buy Baptist"?

By what strange quirk of the human mind have we thus confused our economic conceptions by these irrelevancies?

Mr. De Valera's electoral success will raise a curious question in this connection. He will want all the economic preference that he can get, and while persuading the Irish that Ireland is completely independent of Britain, that he has undone the conquest, that Ireland is standing on her own feet, he will try to persuade the British Government that he is still within the Empire or the Commonwealth; that he is not a foreigner. Well, what makes him a foreigner

from the point of view of Empire preference?
Lord Beaverbrook tells us that we must not
develop trade with the Argentine, because the
Argentine is "outside the Empire," and that
every shilling we spend on Argentinian meat is
just so much taken from the wages of the British
land-worker. What will put Ireland in the
economic sense "outside the Empire"? The
difference between having Ireland inside the
Empire and out seems to be the difference of an
oath, a form of words. In that case there is
something here which outdoes in magic all the
incantations of the past. Ireland, or Mr. De
Valera, pronounces a form of words, an incantation, and forthwith it becomes advantageous
for Britain to buy her goods, to make preferential
arrangements with her; the purchase of Irish
bacon no longer throws English land-workers
out of a job. But if that incantation is not pro-
nounced, every pound of Irish butter or bacon
that is bought represents so much in wages taken
from a British labourer. If, however, Mr. De
Valera will only say those words, the wages are
not taken from the British labourer; they remain
in the British pocket.

The powers of the old magician? We have the
powers of old magical incantations beaten to a
frazzle, as the late President Roosevelt would
have said.

In applying the medical analogy used so plenti-
fully in these lectures, I have asked this question:

Why is it relatively so easy to induce the layman in the West to apply sanitary measures for the prevention of pestilences and all but impossible in the East? In reply, I have suggested that it is certainly not because the Oriental is less intelligent than the Westerner, or more slow-witted; nor because we have "taught" medicine in the schools of the West, because we haven't; but because the Easterner has a certain way of thought, a certain fatalistic attitude towards physical phenomena which we in the West have abandoned. But while we have abandoned that attitude in respect of physical phenomena, we have retained in our attitude towards the facts of human society and human behaviour, with the result that we have the same difficulty in applying political and economic sanitation in the West that in the East they have in applying medical. I am suggesting that unless education can somehow touch this fundamental philosophy of life in the West, no increased knowledge of detailed facts will enable us to control the chaos, no cure that the expert may discover can be applied.

This is revealed plainly enough when we come to deal with the most fundamental sanitary measure of all for the prevention of economic pestilence; the correction of a dislocation we must correct if there is to be any hope of restoring prosperity, the dislocation, that is, which comes from utter anarchy in the international field. How far-reaching, affecting the most highly educated quite as much as the less schooled of our people, is a

certain basic way of thought; how much it stands
in the way of political sanitation, and how
nearly it resembles the Eastern way of thought,
may be indicated by two recent typical examples
of it, to which I took occasion to reply.

Major Yeats-Brown wrote recently in the
Spectator:[1]

I do not believe in the possibility of eliminating the desire to
fight from humankind because an organism without fight is dead
or moribund. Life consists of tensions: there must be a balance
opposite polarities to make a personality, a nation, a world,
or a cosmic system such as God planned. I believe that He
planned war, just as He planned electricity or the force of gravity,
but left it to man to canalize and regulate these powers so that
they should be beneficent rather than destructive. We can support
a League of Nations, but we must not, in our arrogance, imagine
it superior to the Will of Creation: we might as well try to do
away with gravity because of aeroplane accidents as think of
abolishing war because good women suffer and brave men die. . . .

The flower of patriotism has been watered by the blood of
heroic men and women, whereas the weedy hothouse plant of
Geneva has been nourished chiefly on talk and self-interest.
For the desire of nationhood is the germ of life itself. Perfect and
perpetual peace seems to me to lead to stagnation, sterility and
psychic suicide.

A little later Lord Dunsany wrote in the same
journal:

We have no record that when Newton discovered the law of
gravity he incurred any hostility from angry folk saying: Now
we shall have everything falling on our heads, apples and everything else. So I hope my theory will cause no annoyance either . . .
war comes from tides in human affairs, and depends little on
human precautions. Shall we stop it by keeping the birth-rate

[1] December 30, 1932.

down to the level of the death-rate, thus preventing its logical cause? I think not, for that is only to invite invasion. War has been hitherto the method whereby the blood of people was blended, always with a strong tincture of adventure, and whereby races were made. It has been the method whereby those races held their own so long as they were worthy to hold it, and whereby they were overthrown before they cumbered the earth and lowered the average human standard. I like it less than Newton liked being hit on the head by an apple, but I recognize it as one of the conditions under which we live on the planet. . . .

Yet let us hope that the court of King Canute now sitting by the shores of Geneva will stop these tides for ever.

These are merely typical of a mass of literature which reveals the fundamentally fallacious way of thought to which I have referred, and which still pours out. I have tried to isolate the under-lying fallacies, and enumerate them thus:

(1) "*Pacifists forget human nature.*" "Man," say the militarists, "is innately pugnacious, quarrelsome; fight is in his bone and blood." "And that," replies the Pacifist, "is precisely why we must have a League of Nations, an international constitution; the only reason. For if man were not like that, if he were by nature peaceful, able always to see the other's point of view, never lost his temper and called it patriotism, a League would be quite without meaning, and the efforts to create it quite unnecessary. We should not need an international constitution. But neither should we need national constitutions, legislatures, laws, courts, police, churches, ten commandments. These are all conscious efforts to deal with the social shortcomings of human

nature. With the shrinkage of the world, the time has come to add to these traffic rules on humanity's highway." What the militarist deems to be the fundamental argument against Pacifism is the fundamental argument *for* it. I, for one, am a Pacifist, not because I think war unlikely, and men naturally peaceful, but because I believe men to be naturally quarrelsome and war extremely likely. The militarist argument runs: Men like to drive their motor-car as the mood takes them; therefore we must not have traffic rules. The Pacifist argument runs: Men like to drive as the mood takes them; that is why we must have traffic rules. This is the *pons asinorum* of the militarist.

(2) *But you cannot change human nature.* No one proposes to change human nature (whatever that may mean) but to change human behaviour; which all instructed psychologists every day experience, all history, show can be changed enormously by conditions, institutions, tradition, moral values, suggestion, education, as witness certain slight changes in the matter of cannibalism, human sacrifice, polygamy, slavery, the burning of heretics, the torture of witnesses, the duel, and a thousand commonplaces of daily life. If the phrase about human nature is altered to "You cannot change human behaviour," how does one explain the vast changes just indicated in the daily life of the West?

(3) *War has biological roots; marks the need of expanding populations for room;* is the ultimate "struggle for bread."

Compare this theory, paraded so often as "realism," with the facts of the world about us, a world in which every nation is trying its utmost not to seize the food and resources of other nations, but to *keep them out* by insurmountable tariff walls, a fantastic world in which we go in terror, not of scarcity, but of plenty; where a considerable proportion of its population stands idle by idle machines, because it has not yet learned how to distribute the food it already produces. Brazil burns coffee; Canada burns wheat, but neither burns the coal of the British miner, who goes without both the coffee and the wheat. The trouble is plainly due to dislocation, a failure of world co-ordination, co-operation, a failure so great as to produce a chaos in which we may starve in the midst of potential opulence. The dislocation, the defective co-operation which produces this inability to use the abundance which lies at our feet, cannot be cured by war, for its main direct cause has been war, and by the spirit which underlies war. The truth is not "Fight or starve," but "Stop fighting or starve." The cure for insufficiency is better co-operation, and war makes better co-operation impossible. Half a million Indians, divided into numberless tribes, perpetually at war found the whole of what is now the United States inadequate for sustenance, and often starved. The same territory later supports two hundred times that population at an infinitely higher standard—because they managed to keep peace among themselves. If a dozen nations within the British Islands had gone on fighting each other, the population to-day would enjoy the standard of life of the Heptarchy or the Red Indian. The killing of the Indians by the Whites was only inevitable in the sense that Al Capone or lynching is inevitable; the experience of Penn, Las Casas, and a host of others, to say nothing of the Canadian Government of to-day, proves that old and new populations can live side by side without war. Because Queen Elizabeth financed piracy and the slave-trade, it is not "inevitable" that George V should follow suit in our opening up of Africa.

(4) *War is necessary to change the status quo.* If and when Mr. De Valera proclaims his Republic, shall we declare war? I venture to doubt it, for "unchanging human nature" behaves very differently in 1933 from what it would have done in 1913. The same people who for two generations had passionately, bitterly resisted Home Rule, many of whom would have resisted Asquith to the point of civil war, grant only a few years later the vastly greater autonomy of Dominion status without turning a hair. It constitutes a change in the *status quo*. The *status quo* has been changed again and again without war. Canada gets readily what the Thirteen Colonies had to fight for.

(5) *War is productive of many fine qualities.* So is the smallpox epidemic. But we have decided, on balance, against the pestilences of the past. Whatever the advantages of the Black Death may have been (and they were many) we have

decided that we don't intend to have a repetition. That decision, that we don't want pestilence and are prepared to pay some price for preventing it, was the first indispensable step to its abolition. But the militarist has not decided what he wants. He *says* he wants peace; and then immediately disparages it. ("Psychic suicide.") Which brings us to the practical importance of this fatalist philosophy, embodied in the final dogmatic assertion.

(6) *War is inevitable.* Perhaps. I do not know. Nobody knows. Does it mean that any war proposed at any time by any interested party— silly and irresponsible newspapers, demagogic politicians, armament firms—is inevitable? Of course not. Then which war is inevitable and which avoidable? Not a few historians and statesmen have declared that the existence of a League of Nations in 1914 would have prevented this war. If we cannot be sure of that, neither can we be sure of the contrary.

Though we do not know whether "war" is inevitable, we do know that disease is inevitable. Yet, in the West, plague, cholera and leprosy have been wiped away. Is that no gain? It is a gain which we could not possibly have made if men had said: "Pestilence is inevitable. It is fate. What can our poor human wills do against fate—and perhaps Providence. These scourges must be accepted as one of the conditions under which we live on the planet. And who knows, they may be a cleansing tide." I say that we would never have fought pestilence if that fatalism had dominated us, because where that philosophy does dominate, as in certain areas of the East, these pestilences still rage. They rage because many Orientals look upon sanitary protection exactly as the militarist in the West looks upon the efforts of Pacifists and internationalists: the tiresome interference of fussy busybodies, professing with their chatter to hold back tides that have poured over the world since the world began. In the face of that fatalism Western sanitation is impotent to do what with another philosophy can be done; as the facts of the West prove.

A similar fatalism in the presence of that ancient pestilence of war will produce a similar impotence. But it won't be an inevitable impotence, as in the presence of storm or earthquake. Men do not make the earthquake, and have no responsibility for it. They do make war. Army budgets do not get voted and battleships built by "nature" nor by "fate." Men do the voting and the building and the firing; and must not shunt off the responsibility on to "fate" or "destiny" or "nature."

No one pretends that it will be easy to ensure peace. It will be impossible if every effort to that end is disparaged, treated with contempt and sneers. That attitude, if general, will spell failure: failure because we so willed it. The responsibility will be man's, not nature's. Nor God's.

I have gone into this matter of the relation of human nature to human institutions, not primarily as an argument against war, which is not the subject of these lectures, but because the intellectual confusion involved is, so long as it continues, an insurmountable barrier to the creation of a workable world; it is a confusion which prevents us finding the way of escape from chaos. Incidentally we shall get nearer to the abolition of war if we conceive of that problem, not as the negative one of stopping something, but as a constructive one of creating a just, workable, stable international society. If we can get such an international society, the problem of war will almost solve itself. The causes which make our world unworkable, which create the chaos, are those which create war.

The philosophical fallacy with which I have just dealt is extremely simple—almost as simple and self-evident as the economic fallacy which results in the demand for "money, not goods," from America to us in the matter of Debts or from us to Germany in the matter of Reparations.

How is it that our education somehow misses clarification on such vital and fundamental points? No learning, no knowledge, however great, can keep us straight if we get these things wrong— and great learning on the multitude of matters with which modern life deals is in any case impossible for the million. It would seem to suggest that a little more emphasis might be directed first of all towards these great simplicities.

Here are very broad conceptions which we get wrong, points at which poisonous microbes enter the mind and start economic pestilences. It is far better, and far easier, I suspect, to prevent the initial misconceptions than to attempt to fill the mind of future voters with odds and ends of facts in economic geography or industrial history—memorizing the products of Brazil or the price of English wool in the fourteenth century. Even though we had millions of these separate facts, the knowledge would not save us from the pestilence if our fundamental attitude of mind were of the kind described; or if the unperceived motive in shaping our policy was, not the welfare of our people—the provision of ample daily bread and shelter—but the desire for that mystic "independence" about which the nationalist talks; or the desire to do foreigners an injury if we could; if, in other words, we do not really know what we want.

Which brings us to the fact that there is a question even simpler and more fundamental than those just discussed, which must be answered before any sound solution is possible, or knowledge be of use to us. It is a very old question; one of which Socrates reminded us, but of which we evidently need to be reminded over and over again. The question is this: Have we made up our minds what we really want of governments and organized society? Plainly, until we have answered that question, study and education are little good, because we do not even know what it is we want to know, and to what ends our efforts shall be directed. It seems to flout common sense to say that we have not yet made up our minds what we want of politics and government. But I think I shall show you that the statement, nevertheless, is true. It is an aspect of our subject with which I propose to deal in our next lecture.

III

DO WE KNOW WHAT WE WANT?

IF you were to ask an ordinary voter what he was aiming at with his party organization, his elections, his votings, the makings and unmakings of governments, he would tell you doubtless that of course he wanted the safety and welfare of his country, security in his means of livelihood, prosperity, the abolition of unemployment, and, at present, to find just that "way of escape" from the economic crisis which the last lecturers of this Foundation were trying to help him to find.

He will be quite sincere when he makes that statement. But I suggest that when he actually does vote and stand for one policy as against another, he quite forgets these conscious rationalized ends, and that what determines his conduct as a citizen is the satisfaction of ends of an entirely different character. In other words, he has not become conscious of what motive he is really obeying, what end he is pursuing; if he were conscious of that end, usually he would not want it. For assuredly he is not trying to get prosperity, economic security, the abolition of unemployment. I think that when he stops to think he wants those things most. But normally unexamined impulses dictate his conduct and lead to the pursuit of contradictory ends. Very

often in politics his more sober and more deliberate purpose is frustrated by other purposes
which he does not so clearly recognize.

An incident of that 1918 election, to which I
have already referred, will illustrate the point:

It was a big election meeting, and both candidates were to address it. It was held at a time
when already the Press had begun to set up a
clamour to make Germany pay the whole cost of
the war. One paper of a million a day circulation
was keeping up day after day an incessant scream:
"He has not said it; he has not said it," the "he"
being Mr. Lloyd George, and "it" being the
statement that he would make Germany pay the
whole cost of the war. At this meeting, the first
candidate, with some sense of responsibility,
began to deal with the point. He tried to show
that you could not make Germany pay the whole
cost of the war; that as payment would have to
be in goods or services, these would constitute
such a flood as to disorganize our own industry
and trade; that the usual free-trade arguments
here did not apply, since there would be no
counter-balancing outgoing of goods, and the
process would be bound to create a dislocation
fatal to the smooth working of the whole economic
machine. It was not a difficult argument to make;
it was extremely simple. But from the first it was
plain the audience would have nothing of it.
There were protests, cat-calls, heckling, and
finally a forceful, bull-necked person towards the
back of the hall sprang up in his seat, and shaking

his fist at the speaker, said: "Look 'ere, drop this rubbish and tell us whether you mean to 'ang the Kaiser and make Germany pay the whole cost of the war. Yes or no?" Again the speaker tried to show that the attempt to make Germany pay would be disastrous to Britain. But the audience immediately set up the cry, "Yes or no! Yes or no! Yes or no!" Finally the speaker had to abandon any attempt to address the audience. His opponent rose. A wily politician, most obviously. He began with a declaration: "I am for hanging the Kaiser." And there followed a recitation of all the German atrocities during the war. He knew them all. He must have specialized on atrocities. Immediately the whole atmosphere changed. The audience, which before had been irritated, resentful, or bored, sprang to life. Cheer after cheer greeted his declarations concerning the punishment of the Huns and his recital of atrocities. When he sat down there was no doubt as to who would get the votes. He did get them, was elected, making part of what a Tory Prime Minister has called "the house of hard-faced men who looked as though they had done mighty well out of the war."

Now in that speech which carried him to Parliament, there was not one word from beginning to end which bore even remotely upon the welfare of Great Britain. It was the first speech—which the audience howled down—that dealt with that subject. The second speaker knew perfectly well that, in fact, the audience was not interested in the prosperity of Great Britain. What they wanted was the satisfaction of hungry emotions, of a desire for retaliation. The astute politician gave them what they wanted.

It is true, of course, that in a more sober moment this vast audience wanted good wages, safe employment, protection from the miseries and tragedies of unemployment, the welfare of their children, good housing, education. But they also wanted to satisfy this passion of retaliation, and had not learned the trick of sorting out their wants, as it were, of keeping the two things apart; they lost, during that election, all sense of what governments are really for—if, that is, we assume governments *are* for the purpose of ensuring the prosperity of the country they govern.

I suggest that it ought not to be beyond the wit of the educationalist to develop the habit first of a certain type of elementary introspection, a habit which prompts one, on doing a thing like casting a vote, to say to oneself: "Now what is it really that I want?" and secondly, the habit of choosing one's occasions for a little healthy savagery, so that one is able to see that although it may be very satisfactory and necessary at times to indulge our emotions, the ballot-box is not the place to do it; that the making and unmaking of governments is not for the purpose of entertainment or emotional satisfaction, but for clearly conceived ends of national welfare. Again, if this association of ideas is not commoner than it is, it is largely because there is deliberately cultivated in the schools an attitude which in one way or another makes that type of intellectual discipline impossible.

Let me give an illustration—which I have used a good deal because it is a simple one—of the way in which Electorates (*a*) fail to ask themselves what they want, what governments are for, and (*b*) fail, for that reason, in their public decisions to use the knowledge they already possess.

Some years ago I found myself a parliamentary candidate, having undertaken the task mainly perhaps from the desire to become a little better educated politically by meeting Public Opinion face to face, as it were, and not merely through the printed word.

Tackling the job as seriously as possible, my first step was to seek expert advice as to the proper nursing of a constituency from one who was reputed to be quite the astutest electioneer in the country. In reply to my various questions as to the best method of winning the "great heart," he delivered a little lecture which ran about as follows:

You might take Willoughby, who sits for a constituency not far from that which you propose to fight, as a model of really successful electioneering. He has the safest seat in England, in a constituency which used to be very fickle. He has made himself absolutely secure. How? I will tell you. He sits as you know for Birchampton—a sizable industrial city. Now you may know also that that city happens to be the birthplace of Miss Tottie Trixie, the music-hall star. The town is inordinately, absurdly proud of her; they are people of curious enthusiasms up there and Tottie is one of them. There is not a newsboy that would not know her by sight, would not greet her by her Christian name.

Very well. The first step in Willoughby's astounding political success was to marry that actress. It proved a tremendous electoral asset of course. It is important to realize why, if you want to understand the underlying forces in electioneering. The great objective in an election is to get into personal and sympathetic touch with those who might vote against you. It is easy enough to get enthusiastic meetings of your own supporters. But that won't help you very much: they would vote for you anyway. The thing to do is to reach the other side in some way: to let them see that you are a human being, and a decent sort of chap after all. Well, Willoughby could always get the other side to come to his meetings. Why? Because his wife, the famous Tottie Trixie, was always there on the platform, making, indeed, most of the speeches and giving an entertainment as good as she gives at the Follies. Whenever Willoughby holds a meeting, the whole town, quite irrespective of political opinion, turns out to it. And she really is rather amusing and has a most taking "way with her." Why, those present, even if they don't like Willoughby's politics, remember that after all he is the husband of the most famous woman Birchampton ever produced—and the prettiest in England. And that's only the beginning. You know the man's military record? He killed seven Germans with his own hands, a fact of which Tottie never fails to remind the audience and of which he could not very well remind the audience himself. And something still more important. Willoughby is a big upstanding fellow (stupid as a wooden image, but a great athlete). Well, he does not confine his interest in the City football team to ceremonial kick-offs at matches; he becomes an actual member of the team and plays exceedingly well, and on one crucial occasion when a cup-tie decision was involved managed to kick three goals against Manchester United. That of course put the lid on it. After that the election became a mere formality. A seat which his party could never count on holding has become a walk-over for *him*. Turn that man out of Birchampton? Not on your life. Whoever attempts it is going to fail. Tottie will see to that.

My informant may have pulled my leg a little in his somewhat too picturesque attempt to drive home his points. But will anyone who knows anything of politics deny that factors something like those he enumerated weigh enormously in the normal electoral fight?

Let us see what such a story means with reference to the generalization of a moment ago—that the commonest error made by the public in its political decisions is to ignore the self-evident fact, the truth of which it is perfectly well aware; that sometimes the worst errors into which nations fall are self-evident errors, plain to the least-informed intelligence, if intelligence of any kind is applied.

Those elections that placed the footballer in his seat happened at a time when Britain was going through the gravest crisis, perhaps, the country had known since the Industrial Revolution, perhaps the gravest crisis it has ever known. The country's capacity to feed its population at all, its position in the world, the kind of life that the next generation would lead, its liability to new wars, to unemployment of the acutest kind, to poverty, low wages, appalling housing conditions, were all involved in those elections. Every vote was important. The need for getting all possible support for the right policy as against the wrong was vital.

Well, what weighed with ten or twenty thousand adult men and women at that time of crisis in that particular constituency? What really

weighed was the fact that one of the candidates
had married a pretty actress, had killed seven
Germans, and had kicked three goals.

Did they really know what they wanted? Did
they really want the cure of unemployment,
improvements in the monetary system, better
economic organization?

And if that is what they wanted, what shall
we say of an education which leads them to
suppose that the capacity to marry actresses, kill
Germans, kick goals is the proper qualification
for dealing with problems of foreign trade,
inflated or deflated currency, public debt, better
housing and the appeasement of Europe? I suggest
that somehow education had failed to develop
the type of introspection which makes it possible
to avoid this kind of diversion from deliberately
determined ends; or to develop the aptitude
which enables us to apply to new situations as
they arise the knowledge we already possess. The
one fact which was plain, undoubted, self-evident,
was the one fact which in the case cited was
completely disregarded. The minds of the
thousands fell into the trap of a quite irrelevant
sympathy; not a sympathy bad in itself, good,
indeed, in itself, but disastrous, catastrophic, when
allowed to determine decisions to which it is
completely irrelevant when used to justify escape
from reason.

In the political and social field, more perhaps
than in any other, do men go astray by forgetting
to remind themselves "what it is all about"—for

what purpose, that is, they organize society at
all; create governments. If you ask an ordinary
man what he wants of politics, he will tell you that
he wants as secure and full a life for himself and
his dependents as possible: welfare, freedom,
freedom particularly from racking economic
anxiety, from unemployment; stability, secure
old age. He is sure, he tells you, that he wants
these things of politics. But the passionate outbursts of nationalism, the nursing of historical
animosities which so often determine elections,
the considerations influencing political development in Germany and France sufficiently prove
the contrary. During the Presidential election the
editor of the *New York Nation* bewailed the fact
that the American elector, in the matter of debts,
was putting his hates in front of his interests,
that it was so much easier for a politician to
exploit national animosities than to appeal to
interest.[1] It is almost always so in elections everywhere. Mr. Frank Simonds declares in his book
that the Paris settlement was due "to the existence of a spirit which then and in the following

[1] "Even the most cold-blooded banker does not refuse to examine
his debtor's capacity to pay. He does not shout at his debtor, as so
many Congressmen are now shouting: 'Pay or repudiate—all or
nothing!' He is not primarily anxious to humiliate his debtor, to
call him a welcher, to pick a fight with him, to cut off any possible
future friendly relations with him. He is primarily anxious that his
debtor be kept going, so that that debtor will be both able and willing
to repay him as much as he can. This would be the attitude of our
Congressmen if they were thinking merely of our self-interest; but
the utterances of many of them make it clear that they are actuated
to an astonishing extent by pure malice and hatred, no matter how
costly those sadistic emotions may be to us" (*The New York Nation*).

years placed racial and national aspirations above all considerations of economic prosperity and financial stability."

A week or so before the Irish election the *Spectator* said:

The strength of Mr. De Valera's position rests essentially on his appeal to national sentiment. Mr. Cosgrave appeals to national interest. The latter has the immense advantage of having something tangible to offer, and likely to be immediate in its good effects.

But it was no particular advantage, for, as *The Times* on the morrow of the election remarked:

Mr. De Valera owes his position to a traditional hatred of England . . . among new voters of both sexes with more knowledge of Irish historical grievances than of Irish—or any other —economics.

The Balkanization of Europe has not been produced by any thought about interest. It has been produced by feeling about hostilities. If thought about interest were the dominating factor, Europe would have unified itself long before this. It has at this moment two choices: unification and prosperity, or disruption and poverty. There seems every indication that it will choose poverty.

We may well be choosing it within Great Britain. Mr. De Valera's example seems to be catching. Reports are that the Scottish nationalism grows. Scottish nationalists of to-day may not desire to make Scottish nationalism what Irish nationalism has become, to associate it, that is, with a new tariff barrier, economic self-sufficiency, and the rest of it. But the successors of the present Scottish nationalists will certainly insist upon self-sufficiency, tariff barriers. (The predecessors of Mr. De Valera did not insist upon those things.) So probably we are in for a new tariff barrier on this island itself. And then, of course, as I reminded you in the last lecture, will be the turn of Wales. The Welsh nationalist assures you that he is not dreaming of barriers, but Parnell and Redmond did not want them either. Their successors imposed them. And after Wales, if only the philologists can revive ancient Cornish, we shall get a new national unit there. "Cornwall for the Cornish. Buy Cornish."

The supreme case, if we had the imagination to see it, of not knowing what we want is revealed by contrasting what we declared to be the purpose of the war and attitude to that purpose after the war.

The war was to vindicate, we said, the principle of democracy; it was a fight against autocracy. The opening sentence of a five-volume *History of the Peace Conference in Paris*, edited by H. W. V. Temperley, and published under the auspices of the Institute of International Affairs, is as follows:

The war was a conflict between the principles of freedom and of autocracy, between the principles of moral influence and of material force, of government by consent and of government by compulsion.

Popular writing was even more emphatic still on this point. No sooner is the war over than a veritable epidemic of dictatorships breaks out in Europe and nobody much minds. Although Mussolini has more of autocracy in his little finger than the Kaiser had in his whole body, Mussolini is, with millions who supported the war on the ground that we had to make the world safe for democracy, far more popular than the Kaiser was. Hitler really does stand for personal dictatorship which the Kaiser did not, and not once have I seen a comment in our Press to the fact that his appearance as Chancellor is in fact evidence that the purpose of the war —if indeed democracy was its purpose—has utterly failed.

The other purpose we proclaimed was a new international order. The contrast is even greater because in this objective the national policy of our own state, by reason of its diplomatic and political influence, would be decisive. We declared again and again that we were fighting to create a new kind of world politically. We had no real feeling for this because we had no real understanding of its significance.

The public, as a whole, are quite ready to agree that, "in the abstract," the processes by which we live are international; that our economic system, particularly in its necessary financial apparatus, has been proved, again and again, to be incurably so; that any aggravation of economic nationalism makes things worse, and that our first need is international agreement and co-ordination on certain points.

All this is accepted readily enough when a business or political leader lays it down—or did, e.g. the Prince of Wales the other day, in a most admirable speech,[1] when he ended by an appeal for "trained intelligence" to be brought to that task.

Is it "trained intelligence" which determines the policies we apply in this connection? I suggest that we have not really learned to choose in this matter between our impulses in public policy.

When the Prince thus spoke of world-wide interdependence as of the very essence of the modern economic system, the business men he was addressing cheered lustily. But they cheer very nearly as lustily when Lord Beaverbrook

[1] In addressing a Conference on Business Education, he said:
"We have all been learning through the surest and hardest of lessons—adversity—how closely the prosperity of all nations of the world depends upon the prosperity of each and all of them. In these days of swift transport and communication and of interlocked commerce and finance, it is more than ever true that nations cannot live to themselves alone. That the truth is penetrating the minds and governing the policies and actions of nations in growing measure has recently been demonstrated most happily at Lausanne."

Moreover, the Prince dotted i's and crossed t's, pointing out why international co-ordination and organization is necessary.

"The world-wide trade depression and economic disturbance from which we all suffered so much has been largely caused by maladjustment of distribution and consumption of the world's capacity for production. The potential output of the existing means of production in the world is far greater than ever before. If all the employable labour were employed for a reasonable number of hours per week, the world would have at its disposal a volume of commodities and services that would enable the entire population to live on a higher level of comfort and well-being than has ever been contemplated in the rosiest terms of the social reformer.

"The urgent task for the world is to bring about the adjustment necessary to bring consumption and production into proper relationship—not a simple not an easy, but quite a possible task."

tells them the exact contrary, tells them that it does not matter how much foreign trade we lose, "because there is the Empire"; that the rest of the world can go hang; that "this international-ism" is all bunk, and that the League of Nations ought to be scrapped. If a proportion of the business men thus instructed are more than a bit dubious, the great multitudes who continue to read the Beaverbrook Press seem to see no contra-diction between what they read therein and what they cheer when the Prince of Wales or Mr. Baldwin or the Prime Minister addresses them. There seems to be no faintest realization that if what the Prince has been saying about the world and the League and his country's position is really true (and it happens to agree with what men like Sir Arthur Salter, Sir Walter Layton, Sir Josiah Stamp, Sir William Beveridge, and a host of others, who have devoted their lives to the study of the subject, tell us), then Lord Beaverbrook is engaged in destroying our coun-try's security and prosperity, in a work of infinite danger and mischief.

The "average sensual man" (a schoolboy once, fittingly enough, translated the French phrase "l'homme moyen sensuel" as "the mean sensual man"), while vaguely approving peace and ap-plauding internationalism "in the abstract," will also deride the only means by which it can be carried into effect, for the reason that he dislikes the League, Pacifists, and all organized efforts towards peace, for the same reason that he dis-

H

likes Teetotallers, Prohibitionists, Vegetarians, Sabbatarians, Reformers, for both groups alike convey to his mind the impression of an attempt still further to limit his freedom in a world where pagan freedom is scarce enough. Even though the average man would not in fact want to get nationalistically drunk and punch the heads of people he does not like, most of us possess an obscure pagan instinct which makes us want to preserve the *right* to do these things. In the case of those who have some sense of the danger that encompasses the world, some understanding of what the League means as the only thing which can save us from a chaos of futilities, meannesses, falsehoods, miseries which will debase and darken life, the desire to achieve the real liberation which a strong League would ensure, simply sweeps away the rather muddled desire to retain anarchy because heads can then be punched.

But the preoccupied millions—the tired farm-labourer, the squire wrestling with the problems of his insolvent estate, the tea shop waitress, or comedy actress, or the hostess exhausted with the season's activities—do not (let us be honest) understand the issue between the League method and the old method; have not worked out clearly the relative risks of the two. They don't want war, heaven knows. But neither do they want interfering foreigners sticking their noses into our affairs; nor do they see why we should stick our noses into theirs. Isn't it common sense for each to attend to his own business? And when someone tells them that the League is costing a hundred and fifty thousand a year (or was it millions?) he will certainly applaud disparagement of it.

The real reply to this campaign has, curiously enough, also been made by the Prince of Wales. In a recent speech at a League of Nations Union dinner, His Royal Highness, referring to those who, in all countries, "profess to have no belief in the efficacy of the League of Nations to prevent another devastating world war," put this question:

If they mistrust the League, what possible alternative have they to offer for establishing peace and rebuilding prosperity?

And, of course, they have no alternative. Indeed, their position is that there *can* be no alternative, for they tell you, "you can never stop war, because you can't stop human nature"—or get over German wickedness, or French obstinacy, or whatever the prevailing catch-phrase of the moment may be. Those who now rampage against the League do not have to offer an alternative because they do not deal in arguments; they deal in feelings, tempers; they exploit human exasperation, natural impatience with the world's confusion; and an impatience at any implied restraint. This campaign is an invitation to irritated people to curse the most unpopular person or thing in sight; unpopular, not because of vices, but because he or it is "superior."

We all knew that the creation of any workable alternative to the old system would be a particularly tough job. On one condition only could it have any chance of success: that we should have the will to make it a success, be in earnest about it, take trouble about it. *No* difficult thing can succeed save on that condition.

But the Beaverbrooks and Rothermeres have never permitted that one condition of success. At first the League was damned with faint praise, and since then derision has been piled on criticism and—sometimes—sheer falsehood (as in the "expense" argument) on derision. Never has this particular type of newspaper taken any part in creating the will to succeed in this peace effort as they helped to create the will to succeed in war. It is not merely that they object to the League; they object to any departure from the old system of competitive armament. Both the Rothermere and Beaverbrook papers oppose and deride the Disarmament Conference (which includes America and Russia) as bitterly as they oppose the League. It is all one to them. They object to the Disarmament proposals of America, of Germany, of Russia, as much as they object to those of France or Britain. They will tell you, of course, that they want peace. What they object to is any organized efforts towards getting it. Any departure at all from the old system of competing national armament is to be derided as fantastic and ridiculous.

It is all such a very old story, so universal and so ridiculous. Lords Beaverbrook and Rothermere shout that they will not have anything to do with the League because it is a French institution; M. Coty shouts that Frenchmen must not have anything to do with it because it is a British one; Mr. Randolph Hearst shouts that Americans must have nothing to do with it because it was invented by sly Europeans to entrap innocent Americans; and Herr Hugenburg (or Herr Hitler) shouts that it was invented by the Allies for the permanent subjugation of Germany. And as to Disarmament, each is prepared to prove that his own nation has simply stripped itself of arms, while foreigners have gone on increasing their arms as the direct consequence.

Insincere? One almost wishes that it were. For that would imply some capacity at least to see the facts, to examine the advantages in terms of welfare and security, which each country is to derive from this crazy mass of contradictions. The nationalist may tell you that he wants the welfare and security of his country; but what he really wants is the satisfaction of certain emotions that have nothing to do with those things. The French anti-Dreyfusard told us that he was fighting for the safety and honour of France; but the whole non-French world saw that he was pursuing a policy the plain effect of which was to dishonour France and undermine her security. It is impossible for one who has listened to anti-Dreyfusards to read to-day a speech by a Hitlerite without being struck by the fact that the rhetoric is merely the sort of stuff that M. Déroulede or M. Lucien Millevoye used to give us thirty years or so ago, done into German. Mr. De Valera is the embodiment of Irish Nationalism, and his followers will tell you with complete sincerity that his policy is dictated by love of Ireland and concern for its security. Everybody outside his own party sees clearly that the repudiation of the Treaty cannot possibly be to the advantage of Ireland, and is bound to injure alike the credit and the welfare of that country. The motives which push such questions as the Oath and formal separation into the foreground have plainly nothing to do with welfare. Yet those who promote those policies believe they have.

The astounding progress of the Nazi movement (pushed home by the electoral victories in Prussia the other day) illustrates strikingly the point that no argument need be offered where unexamined emotions can be exploited. This tremendous success has been achieved by a party that not only offers no arguments, properly speaking, but no programme. No one knows what the Nazis would really do on coming to power. As *The Times* Berlin correspondent says: It promises everything vaguely and nothing definitely, and its promises usually cancel out each other. Hitlerism is of course merely an acute sense of grievance directed against whatever object the potential adherent of the party may dislike. To the anti-Semite, Hitler offers oppression of the Jews; to the Chauvinist, punishment of the French; to the worker, abolition of the capitalist; to the capitalist, control of the worker through a Fascist government; and so on and so on. And it is noteworthy that this manifestation is staged in Prussia, where education of the scholastic and academic type is more thorough and more widespread than anywhere else in the world, and has been for a century. It is sufficient commentary upon the degree to which modern European education equips the millions for life together in that new kind of world which the last fifty years have brought into being.

The first book I happened to write on international affairs[1] was called in its sub-title "A Plea for Rationalism in Politics"—a plea, that is, for the examination of the motives which push nations into the policies which they pursue. I tried there to show that the motives were often not rational at all, that any consciously conceived end of welfare or happiness was buried in a mass of impulses which not only did not promote welfare but frustrated it. The first case taken as illustration was America's incursion into Imperialism in the Spanish War and the annexation of the Philippines. (The impulse nearly found expression in an American war with us a little previously over the

[1] *Patriotism under Three Flags*, Fisher Unwin, London. The book met with this criticism: "The author is mistaken in assuming that such motives underlie national action; the real motive is economic, the push of economic need." I set about therefore examining *that* motive; all as part of the effort to be clear as to what we were really all trying to do. I felt further that if the destructive character of war were revealed the people might come to the conclusion that though emotional outbursts are great fun, the break-up of civilization is too high a price to pay and that other means of satisfaction could perhaps be found.

boundary of British Guiana.) This was paralleled
with our own outburst in the conquest of the
Boer Republics, and the French outburst over the
Dreyfus case. In these apparently dissimilar events
I thought I saw (journalistic work happened to
have brought me into contact with all three manifestations) a common motive at work—the motive
of power, pride of place, national vanity; not
economic welfare.

Economic motive, obviously, played small part
in the attitude of the populace in France with
regard to the Dreyfus case, a case which displayed
the existence of a political feeling identical with
that displayed by Englishmen in the case of the
Transvaal War, and Americans in the case of the
Spanish War. It was alleged indeed by all the
"patriots" in France that "la haute finance"
threw its whole weight against anti-Dreyfusism—
against all those forces of militarism, aggressive
nationalism, hatred of the foreigner, autocracy
and national vanity, which the world over
make for Imperialism and are part of its policy.
French Nationalism, which in its psychology and
philosophy looked then astonishingly like British
Imperialism, maintained for years a furious campaign, which not merely could have no root in
financial considerations, but which was (incidentally) opposed to all the forces of high finance.

As little could it be claimed that the outburst
which followed Mr. Cleveland's Venezuelan
Ultimatum, and which all but precipitated a
conflict between England and America, was

financially inspired. It may be that the interests of certain financiers were served by the outbreak, but the warlike fury which animated the bulk of Americans at that time was genuine enough. It was impossible to move amongst Americans and to have any other opinion. The manifestation was too sudden and too evidently spontaneous to allow one to suppose it for a moment the result of careful "engineering." To a less degree the same thing held true of the aggression by the United States upon Spain. All the evidence goes to show that the American Government—then as now in intimate contact with financiers—would have avoided war had it not been forced thereto by popular clamour. The commercial interests as represented by the Chambers of Commerce declared for the most part against it. One may well doubt whether the desire to increase the field of investments was the chief motive of the Philippine policy.[1] The careful calculation which such a motive implies on the part of the administration would almost inevitably have brought a recognition of the fact that substantial control of the islands could have been obtained without the formal imposition of American authority. Again, the intensity of sentiment excited in the nation is disproportionate to the material interests involved.

[1] Industrial interests in America, particularly those connected with sugar, have just been using their influence with Congress to force through, against Presidential veto, a bill granting Independence to the Philippines in ten years time. Here is a case in which capitalist interest is running directly counter to annexation, to "Imperialism." The competition of Philippine sugar has prompted the *dis*-annexation of conquered territory.

Millions of Americans were furious expansionists who had not the remotest concern in Philippine investments or exploitation. American capitalists as a whole could find plenty to exploit in their own country, since most of the Western States were still indebted by some millions to European capitalists.

I noted, at the time of Cleveland's Venezuelan message, that though the American farmer stood to lose enormously by conflict with England— whole agricultural communities out West must have been absolutely ruined by such an event— no class was more intensely Anglophobe at the time of the Venezuelan crisis, or more eager for the fray. So in France in the Dreyfus affair. The French common people, with sons and husbands subject to military authority, could have had no interest in endowing the military caste with arbitrary privilege. Yet the common people were as anti-Dreyfusard as the military themselves. I felt this to be in keeping with the underlying motives of most national and racial animosities, of the religious intolerances of the past. While agreeing that economic motive played its part in the religious wars, and in the costly religious persecutions carried on by governments during whole centuries, it was the motive of an interested minority, exploiting powerful popular passions which were not mainly economic. But for the existence of those passions the minority would have found itself powerless. If we are to explain those conflicts purely as conflicts of economic interest, how are we to explain the conduct of those who resisted the persecution? Explanations of material interest hardly hold when we are confronted by the spectacle of a man allowing himself to be burned alive rather than recant a conviction. Indeed, most persecutions derived their force, not from the machinery of government, but from the extent to which they embodied the feeling of the majority, the populace as a whole. The position of the clergy in this matter perhaps illustrates the position of class interests in modern Imperialist movements. It is true that the priesthood of Europe had a material interest in heresy hunting, but the populace had not. To explain religious persecution and bigotry as merely the outcome of class interest is to disregard obvious psychological fact. Religious bigotry—the hatred of a man of one religion for that of another—is a fact in nature with which material interest has obviously at times nothing to do. And of racial animosity, the same is at times obviously true. To quote from myself:

"In the case of religious bigotry, mere difference of opinion, often over matters of ceremonial, which on the surface seem infinitely trivial, can, as we know, stir deep hate, and convulse nations for generation after generation. Indeed, a glance at some of the great religious conflicts of history would seem to justify the generalization that intensity of feeling in a people varies in inverse ratio to the material interest involved. But for this fact, the vested interest of the priesthood

would have been powerless to inspire such events
as the massacre of St. Bartholomew, and to
maintain such institutions as the Inquisition.
Sometimes the persecutions, notably of the Jews,
took place in the teeth of priestly injunction.
The Pope himself was impotent to save the Jews
from popular fury as more than one well-attested
case shows. Religious hatreds are rampant to-day
in spheres outside the range of priest influence.
This fact of bigotry, a sentiment often indulged
at great material cost to the bigot, is only too
evident. Secular history, with its tale of century-
long conflicts, having little other basis than that
of race difference, and often not even that, pro-
vides like illustrations. It is possible that the
Protestant or Catholic, if pushed to justify his
persecution, would allege some overpowering
material or moral interest: the anti-Popery man
declare that he was defending the bulwarks of all
freedom, civil and religious, and the anti-Protestant
that he was protecting society from moral anarchy.
Both pleas would be after-thoughts. The Americans, clamouring for war with England over a
Venezuelan swamp, betimes alleged some motive
of interest and well-being—self-protection, and
I know not what—but that, too, was an after-
thought. The impulse to war had its origin in
something of a different order. Where, again,
the pretext of self-interest cannot be made to
appear on the surface of the case, it will be quite
frankly invented in the same sort of after-thought,
as the anti-Dreyfusard invented the "International

Syndicate of Treason." Where such pretexts as these have any sincerity, they are due to self-deception, itself the result of auto-suggestion.

The analogy of the Catholic clergy utilizing religious bigotry for the advancement of their vested interests suggests sufficiently clearly the relations between patriotism and the vested interests which exploit that sentiment. Both clergy and financier share the prejudices they exploit. The analogy also indicates what should be the attitude of the political or sociological reformer towards Imperialism. Experience shows that it availed nothing to strike at the power of the priest while the mind of the laity was still dominated by religious bigotry. Popular animosity undirected by the priesthood sufficed to stamp out as heresy most that was best and spontaneous in thought; so in our mob-passions, though liberated from financial direction, would still generate insane rivalries, demand domination, and ignore the claims of rational well-being. For the same reason democratic control, however real and effective, would avail nothing while fanatical nationalism possesses the mind of the people. In some cases at least the oligarchic rather than the democratic elements have been our salvation in patriotic crises. It was so in the Venezuelan affair: while the populace clamoured for "stern measures" and decisive action, the American Administration did its best to undo the first mischief. In the Dreyfus case, the same phenomenon. The government were often haltingly for justice, while the populace were demanding oppression.

Above the questions of commerce and material benefit are placed the political ends of rule and dominion. Thus the emphasis the patriot places upon all things touching the power and prestige of the nation, and the relative negligence of the material well-being of the individual citizen. This last is only considered in so far as it may serve the ends of national rivalry, pride of place. The patriot loves his country, but not usually his countrymen.

IV

THE CONDITIONS OF SUCCESSFUL PLANNING

You may read into the theme of these lectures an implication which is not in my own thought. That theme—to remind you of it once more—is that if we could apply the few commonly agreed truths of economic science to our body politic, we should avoid at least some large part of the pestilences which afflict it, and that, if those bad pestilences were so avoided, the remaining sickness would be more manageable.

You may say of this that it is an implication of *laisser faire* and *laisser aller* which are, in these days, very much discredited doctrines, and might go on to point out, perhaps, that the agreed truths, as that the nations should have done immediately after the war what they did at Lausanne, are all passive or negative policies—such as the recommendation not to collect Reparations while maintaining tariffs, or the recommendation not to raise tariffs or indulge in other forms of economic nationalism.

May I say at once that I am a "planner" as opposed to a non-planner, or protagonist of *laisser faire* and *laisser aller*, and would remind you of the application already made of a certain medical analogy, namely, that even if you believe in operations, you can agree that no major

operation is likely to be successful if the patient
happens to be suffering from, say, bad dysentery
at the time, or to be the victim of some grave
infectious disease. And equally if we do *not* believe
in operations for organic trouble, we can agree
that no cure is likely to work if we allow the body
to be subject to cholera, typhus, or bubonic
plague. Such economic efforts as the conscious
adjustment of production to consumption are
condemned to impotence so long as there is
grave monetary dislocation and instability of
the exchanges.

But the theme has an implication which shows
the point at which we must part company with
the medical analogy. One part of my text is that
our problem is not merely to find a way of
escape, but to find a means of enabling the
millions to see that it *is* the way of escape. Note
that I say the millions. It won't do for a small
minority to be persuaded. This is where experiments on the social organism differ from experiments on the physical organism. If a medical
doctor has a new cure, or a surgeon a new operation, and he manages to persuade just one or
two patients to try the cure or the operation,
and it is successful, that success, in just one or
two individual cases, enables the physician to
establish the validity of his cure. But that won't
work in the case of economic and social remedies.
If a man desires to prove that it is better to drive
to the right as they do on the Continent, rather
than to the left, as we do here, he cannot prove

his case by taking his car into the road and driving to the right in England; in order to get an experiment at all, all must drive to the right, or all must drive to the left, and this is true of all the many much recommended economic cures— Communism, Socialism, Fascism, Co-operation, the Distributive State, Protection, Empire Free Trade, Free Trade, a managed currency, a silver standard, a new ratio of the pound to gold, dated currency, unlimited currency for everybody, more taxes, less taxes, more saving, more spending, single tax, no tax. It must be Communism for all or Capitalism for all, as much for non-believers as for believers.

The Communists, of course, recognize this difficulty, and that is largely their case for the dictatorship of a minority. At the bottom of their case for compulsion and coercion lies the un-doubted truth that it is less important, ultimately, whether people drive to the right or drive to the left, than that all should do either one or the other.

But concerning that I would suggest certain things: Firstly, that however indispensable unity of action is, you cannot, in fact, secure it in our complex society by compulsion, for reasons which I will try presently to indicate; secondly, that if issues are clear, the objective plain, to large numbers, no compulsion is necessary, also as I shall try to show presently; and thirdly, that our separation of the "Capitalist system" and the "Socialist" system into supposedly water-tight compartments is artificial and unreal.

I

Take the last point first. We talk of "Capitalism" as being something that is completely and entirely distinct from Socialism or Communism, with no mergence one into the other; as though a Socialist State would have no element of Capitalism, and a Capitalist State nothing of Socialism. Now obviously that is simply not so. Under the very harshest of the doctrinaire Communists, Russia preserved, either at recurrent intervals or regularly, not merely the monetary system, not merely a financial system which included loans and interest, but also at periods and in various ways a large degree of private trading, private profit, private property, private Capitalism as well as State Capitalism. At times it eliminated some of these features of the Capitalist regime only later to return to them. While professing to have rejected the doctrines of gradualism, the Soviet Union has, in fact, applied to a tremendous extent the doctrine of gradualism; and at any given moment the amount whether of Communism or Capitalism in the Russian economy, varies sometimes very greatly from the amount at other times. At some periods there will be a considerable increase of private trading, private property, and a decrease of communal control; and vice versa. This, of course, reveals to my mind political wisdom. But it also shows plainly that with the most convinced, even fanatical, of protagonists of a given economic doctrine like Communism, that doctrine when applied must include a selection from several "systems."

But what is true of Communism is also true, of course, of Capitalism and Individualism. It is sometimes the strongest of individualists who clamours most ardently for the intervention of the State, particularly in the matter of protective tariffs. And as now protection is largely in the form of quotas, we seem to be on the road to developing the very system of bulk purchase by national governments which is, in fact, the Communist system of foreign trade. No one, of course, professes *laisser faire* or *laisser aller*, the absence of government control, that is, for currency, a return to private enterprise in the matter of issuing bank notes, which was a common feature of trade in the eighteenth century. What we have, in fact, seen working, is an eclecticism, Capitalism adopting many Socialist features, and Socialism, when applied, adhering to certain aspects of Capitalism. This, I suggest, is the only possible course of development, the only possible road to control and to planning. Capitalism has ceased to be individualist, is rapidly becoming socialistic; the area of the community's control is extending everywhere, what time Society in Russia is coming to look more and more like Society in the Bourgeois West.

I have implied that if the objective, the general interest, is clear to the mass, vested interests, Capitalist or other, opposed to the general interest soon drop their opposition and fall into line. But the multitude must really know whether it wants prosperity, or the feeding of emotions

like those of Nationalism, or the class war, or
entertainment to be derived from the fight of
parties by the turning of elections into a sort of
football match in which all sorts of irrelevant
preferences are indulged. And as we saw in the
last lecture, the multitude has seldom decided
what its real objective is, what it really wants.

I say that national planning involving large
slices of Socialism need encounter no insurmountable objection on the part of those in
possession because the sort of national management necessary has actually been applied successfully in circumstances of far greater material
difficulty than those which now confront us.

The reference, of course, is to the national
management which we achieved during the war.
The reminder is apt to cause irritation. It is admitted
that we managed miracles of production, but they
were in circumstances, it is added, when cost did
not count in obtaining a market since the Government—ourselves—was the market; that the
method of financing could never have continued
indefinitely; that much of our capital equipment
was disastrously let down, and much more to the
same effect.

But when all the buts are exhausted this fact
remains: if to-morrow we found ourselves at war
with a Great Power, unemployment would disappear: our productivity would not decline, it would
increase; we should, as a matter of course, adopt
measures of control and regulation which we do
not dream of applying to a peace problem; we

should put through legislation to deal with the situation which no peace-time government could pass.

Nor need one expect ever, for any peace purpose, to see duplicated the extent of agreement on radical measures which war produces. But the experience gives us a lead, and certain indisputable truths stand out. Both the possibilities and the difficulties have been put in these terms:

We can, if we will, perfectly well overcome our present difficulties, because, when recently, during the war, we undoubtedly did have the will, we overcame successfully very much worse ones not essentially different in their nature.

We applied instantly, as a matter of course, almost without argument, a principle which marked the effort from the beginning to the end, and which was applied increasingly as the difficulties became greater; and that was the principle of the "national plan," a complete national co-ordination through the authority of the State. The immense majority of British business men in July 1914 would have said—were continually saying, indeed —that the worst way to get things done in the business world was to let the government interfere, or worse still, for Whitehall to try to do it. Well, there came the life-and-death crisis. What, then, was the attitude of these critics of national control? Their conversion took about ten minutes, once they were convinced that the nation's life was involved. They, like the rest, without much argument or objection, acquiesced in the government's taking over everything. It took over the railways in about twenty-four hours; but private business began to follow in about as many weeks, and before many months had passed the government was the nation's merchant, buying and selling, controlling and fixing wages, wool and flour and bacon dealer, and everything else.

But what we could do for ammunition during the war, when, materially, things were most difficult, we could not do for houses after the war, when many of the material difficulties were much less.

Yet all the materials were obtainable within the country itself. (The Americans were already teaching us how far metal could be substituted for wood.) As we had not yet returned to gold exchange, disturbance was of minor importance and no difficult international agreements were involved. Rent restriction had already put into the hands of government a tool which, shrewdly used together with the adaptation of plant for metal production already in its possession, could have given it control of the market for building materials. But the protection of special interests, alike of the capitalist and of certain trade unions, seemed at that time more important than large-scale planning.

At what point and by what method should we have the best chance of re-creating that war-time will to apply conscious control and national planning?

If a Socialist Government were in power as well as office—had a House of Commons majority —what would it do? What should be its policy? The Socialist is liable to look upon such efforts as the meetings of bankers for the stabilization of money, as things which belong to "Capitalism," which hardly concern him, which will come out in the wash on that glorious day when "Socialism" is at last established. Give him the power, the implication usually is, and the rest will follow.

I suggest that power of itself would be ineffective. You may have "power" over your motor-car if you have a crow-bar sufficiently heavy to smash it to pieces. It will not enable you to make it work. The social, economic and financial machine with which we are confronted in Britain is more intricate than any motor-car, with the added complication that it has a will of its own, much of its mechanism resenting the introduction of crow-bars; and it is also suggested that the management of that type of mechanism can only in fact be achieved by the co-operation of the mechanism itself; and that if crow-bars put the mechanism too much out of gear you will be in the position of an aviator flying the Atlantic Ocean whose crow-bar methods with his engine bring him down. The dislocations must be corrected while the machine is running.

It is important in this connection to note how Russian experience may be misinterpreted.

In Russia those faced with the problem of socializing the means of life for the bulk of the Russian people found the problem enormously simplified. The great mass of the people were peasants on a very low standard of life, living by a very primitive agriculture, each village, indeed each family, largely self-sufficient. There was no complicated and delicate organization of industry to be put out of gear by such dislocations as changes in money values, world slumps and the rest. Those factors had some importance, doubtless, even to the Russian peasant family of the most self-sufficient type. But they were not vital. Life could go on even if the cities utterly forgot the peasant's existence: the dislocation of the national machine still left the peasant with means of life. To superimpose industrialization on this simple rudimentary agriculture did not involve the maintenance, meantime, of a highly elaborate financial and economic apparatus: peasants could be induced to drop ploughing with a wooden plough, form themselves into a collectivity and employ in common a tractor, and, later, a combined harvester. There were great difficulties to over-come, of course, but fundamentally the problem was not much more than that.

But socialization for an intricately interde-pendent, urbanized and industrialized civiliza-tion like that of Britain, involved as it is in the obtaining of raw materials on the other side of the world and the sale of manufactures thereto, in varying price-levels, gold distribution, stock exchange speculation, bank rates, foreign debts, a deeply rooted individualist economy—to uproot all this and start it growing again in a quite different way is a task alike in kind and in degree different from that which confronted Russia.

Take two situations in both of which the central governmental apparatus has either broken down or been captured by revolutionary forces, and note the difference. The first case is that of the peasants who had lived heretofore upon a landlord's estates, ground by his exactions, sur-rendering to him a large part of the fruits of their

toil. They can solve the major part of their problem, can transfer to themselves the source of
livelihood in an extremely simple fashion by an
act of physical coercion which demands very
little social co-ordination for its performance.
They can go to the landlord's house, slit his
throat or hang him to a lamp-post, divide up his
land among themselves, and each of them work
his bit for himself without any elaborate social
organization. The more the landlord's State
apparatus has broken down, the easier the transfer
of the source of livelihood, the tangible, visible
and divisible soil, becomes; and the more secure
is the peasants' position, provided that the soil
will support them by simple methods of culture
and each cultivator has learned to be self-sub-
sistent.

In that kind of situation, the condition, that
is, of primitive society, wealth, and means of
production, embodied as they are in cattle,
agricultural tools, land, can be transferred by the
simple process of overcoming physically the
persons in possession of them. But everything is
reversed when you come, say, to the problem of
the workers on a railroad.

They cannot ensure the transfer of that wealth
to themselves by dropping a bomb into the office
of the chairman and board of directors, blowing
them into the air and dividing the railroad
among themselves, each man taking a bit of steel
rail or a coal truck. If wages are to be paid to the
workers at the end of the week, the railroad must

continue to function. This does not mean merely that the workers must be in a position to take over administration and all the technical functions. That of itself would not solve their problem. There must be freight and passengers to carry—which means that the life and activity of the country as a whole must be going on as before. That is, foodstuffs and raw materials like cotton must be imported, and finished products exported, at a price which competes successfully with similar goods being offered from other countries. If links in the long chain are missing; if banking disorganization has compelled the creation of a revolutionary fiat money, or such inflation that higher nominal wages for the railway workers mean in fact much lower wages than before; if the confiscation of securities and the repudiation of loans (which the Communists insist must be "ruthless"—the more ruthless the better, apparently) have so disorganized credit that in fact the purchase of American cotton or overseas foodstuffs cannot be financed; and manufacturing in consequence is so disorganized that foreign sales cannot be effected—then, in that case, there will will not be freights to carry for the railroad, and the workers' "possession" of it avail exceedingly little. The wealth which is the source of life for them is not a material object to be taken by physical coercion from hands that now hold it (which is broadly the case of peasants taking a landlord's estate); it is a very complex process to be maintained, a constantly moving and shifting stream to be diverted from one direction to another, a stream that can only be controlled by the co-ordinated efforts of vast masses of men: railway workers having come to an agreement with coal miners, cotton operatives, printers, dairymen, market gardeners, about prices and conditions; whether unskilled shall get as much as skilled; whether the smallholder must deliver milk at a fixed price or can keep it for raising pigs; whether the market gardener is to have life tenure; whether captains of ships at sea must in this or that circumstance accept the crews' committees. It is clear that in these circumstances the more a State apparatus has gone to pieces, the more difficult will all these co-ordinations become. Individual action here is worthless. It must be collective action, a co-ordination so complex that the co-ordination must in a large degree be voluntary.

Our society is one based on technology; it lives by an elaborate mechanical apparatus that can only be kept going by the work of the technician. If the "class war" came in any near future all the indications seem to point to the fact that the technicians would be overwhelmingly on the Capitalist side of the barricade. A British proletarian dictatorship would probably find even more difficulty in coercing technicians than the Russians found in coercing the peasants—and they found very great difficulty.

We know that the Soviet, after four years of attempted coercion, had to yield to the peasants, yield nearly every item in the Marxian credo, in order to get the indispensable work done. How much of that credo would ultimately have to be yielded to the technicians, alias bourgeoisie, in order to get done the work of reconstruction of a country that has the most complex industrial organization in the world and cannot live for three months without a foreign trade difficult to maintain even in peace-time?

Trotsky, who once wrote of the possibilities of the Revolution in England, said it would be very difficult to overthrow those who now constitute the administrative, technical, specialist and expert sections of the industrial, commercial, and banking apparatus. What does "overthrow" mean? "Elimination," execution, exile, incorporation in the ranks of manual labour? Then the Revolution will be confronted with the task of creating a new personnel of managers, administrators, specialists, experts; not only, of course, for the army, navy, civil service, law courts, the police, and the political services properly speaking, but for the technical direction of such services as transport, shipping, banking, needing currency experts, actuaries, ships' captains and officers, architects, mining engineers, electrical mathematicians, surgeons, doctors, bacteriologists (very necessary when improvised services resulted in confusion between sewage and water mains) —all these from the revolutionary ranks. How long is the creation of such a new order going to take—most available instructors, be it remembered, belonging to the counter-revolutionary party?[1] One generation or several—or only decades? Meantime, one wonders what will be happening to the foreign trade, which alone can bring foodstuffs to Lancashire and the Tyneside.

Let us look at a few facts which would present themselves in a post-revolutionary Britain—facts which neither side for a moment denies—and ask a few questions about them. We are all agreed that the task which would confront the Dictatorship on the morrow of the Social Revolution—that of nation-wide reconstruction along entirely new lines, rejecting the old methods and familiar disciplines which have become almost instincts and invoking new motives for the working of a brand-new apparatus—that such a task would be a stupendous one, and one that could not wait. There would, for instance, be purchases of foreign food and raw materials from foreign concerns to be financed; sales of British produce to be arranged, if Lancashire was to have food next Monday morning. The government would be faced by the immediate need of controlling the very elusive forces that at present are left to control themselves; by problems of price fixing, rationing food, distribution. We are to preserve,

[1] Remembering also that the proletariat will have drawn upon its personnel to replace all the old State apparatus properly speaking —"the old police, the old judiciary, the old army cadets, the old navy officers," as Trotsky reminds us (see *Where is Britain Going?*, pp. 90–103). He seems to hint, indeed, that the "oppressed masses" of India might be drawn upon. A Hindu police would add picturesqueness to the Revolution, whatever its effect upon Trade Union psychology might be.

presumably, the device of money, and not to proceed to its immediate destruction, according to the theory of the early days of the Bolshevik Revolution. But in that case extremely expert management will be demanded if the general confiscation of property of all kinds, the cancellation of loans, the rearrangement of relations between debtor and creditor, employer and worker, bank and State, the foreigner who sells and the British State that now replaces the individual purchaser is not to produce chaos. The preservation, in these circumstances, of balances for the payment of wages or of demands by the State; the prevention of the flight of capital, while preserving sufficient credit abroad—in capitalist countries—to finance the daily purchase of foodstuffs and raw materials; the collection in the midst of complex and puzzling economic changes of new taxes, will all demand reliable, well-trained technicians.

With this situation facing the Dictatorship, to what quarter would it look for the new great bureaucracies that must be improvised, the indispensable technicians—the tax collectors, the accountants, administrators, engineers, ships' captains, banking and currency experts?

The Marxians declare that the constitutional method of change is impossible because the bourgeoisie will fight it with tooth and claw, the power of heaven and the infernal regions. But if that describes the professional man's attitude *before* civil war has taken place, before, indeed, the classes have very clearly formed into "sides," before he has any very clear sense of making part of a corporate body that has scores to pay off, injuries to resent, vengeance to satisfy, what will be his feelings when civil war has sown its dragons' teeth, infected the nation with the venoms, rages, and implacable hates that that kind of struggle always does engender?

And it is at that moment presumably that the Marxians would propose to put much of the administrative machine in bourgeois hands; to put in the hands of this dispossessed class the tools which they could certainly use to sabotage a hated dictatorship, to undermine what they would regard as a bloodthirsty tyranny. In the attempt to make the employment of a class so situated safe from the point of view of the new authority, so much of their demands would have to be conceded that such concession would constitute a return to the policy of gradualness— a policy which, adopted in much less degree before the Revolution, probably would have avoided revolution. The dilemma is quite plain. If the reconstruction is to be rapid, as Trotsky suggests, then it can only be by a widespread employment in direction and administration of the existing professional and middle class, an employment which will put much of the real power under the new order in their hands. If that power is not to be given to them, then recovery will not be rapid. It will be exceedingly slow.

It will be said: It is quite academic to labour

the unworkability of the revolutionary method for Britain, because no one really proposes to apply it. That may be; but the class-war psychology is nursed and tends to make impossible that provisional co-operation of Socialists with the existing system which the policy of gradualness demands for its success. The psychology of the class-war is a poor preparation for co-operation with "the enemy" in that war.

Point out to a member of the Left that such and such a measure would make the whole present system unworkable, and he would be apt to reply: "So much the better." Point out that if there is to be a redistribution of the national income by transferring through taxation part of profits to social services, then industry must be allowed and encouraged to make profit; that such policy is much easier when profits are being made than when they are not and he will deem that you are a heretic to the social faith, since we want to get rid of "production for profit" in favour of "production for service." Which means that he oscillates between the policy of smashing the present system by producing chaos and the policy of transforming it while it is running smoothly.

No one who has had to deal with Labour electorates, at a time when, say, an increase in unemployment benefit is under discussion, will underestimate the seriousness of this difficulty for the Socialist politician. The result of it is that business and industry as a whole is deeply suspicious, does not believe that Socialism of any kind can have any object other than to destroy the present form of industry utterly and reduce those who live by it to penury.

This fundamental misconception or misunderstanding is perhaps the main obstacle to the creation of that psychology which accomplished economic miracles during the war. A thousand times this last ten years it has been pointed out that if we could create for the purposes of peace the same readiness to "plan nationally" that we managed to create during the war; if, say, we could do for houses what we managed to do for munitions, we should have solved our problem, at least in so far as it is a national problem.

But the great difference between war and peace psychology is this: The business man and the industrialist did not believe that the object of all that war-time Socialism was to destroy him; he believed that its object was a national one: the safety and welfare of the British people; that its motive was not wantonly to confiscate his property on behalf of predatory political parties. Of peace-time Socialism he has mainly the idea that its sole object is to do just those things.

We get, then, this: the compulsory method, the revolutionary method, would simply not work in Britain: it would end in chaos or some form of Fascism. But the revolutionary method can destroy.

We get, further, this fact: *laisser faire* has broken

down, and if the industrial and financial machinery is to work there must be conscious control. The machine is neither automatic nor fool-proof. Further, it is misleading to use the term machine: it is an organism which can only be made to function effectively by a measure of its own consent.

But the difficulty is not merely one of securing a general agreement to plan. What is to be the plan?

One generalization which could truthfully be applied to the world of 1933 is this: In the midst of chaos it recognized the need for planning. It finally abandoned in practice, if not in conscious theory, the doctrine of *laisser aller*, and every government in the world proceeded to "plan" in lesser or greater degree and to make some advance to planning on an international scale. The plans often mark revolutionary departures. In America, where heretofore unadulterated individualism has been the unchallenged faith of the whole people, we have seen the government undertaking far-reaching plans of financial regeneration; elaborate economic schemes for the relief of the farmer; and shortly we shall see States embarking upon unemployment insurance, the while the Federal Government is brought nearer to international planning by a less trammelled participation in the World Economic Conference.

In Britain we have abandoned the policy of generations in order to try the plan of a highly

Protectionist Empire—the whole of it tariff-walled against the world and each member tariff-walled against the others. Germany's economy has always been more consciously planned than that of other Western States. Russia continues to pour out successors to the Five-Year Plan; Italy brings forward new ones; while the governments of even little States like Ireland produce "national planning" of truly amazing character.

And as to the plans of regeneration which do not yet come within the orbit of government action, it is a dull week which does not produce something claiming to be at long last the real cure of our discontents. Just now all America is agog with a new one, possessing not only a new name but a new language in which to explain it. From Maine to California, from Michigan to Texas, Americans are discussing "technocracy"; and such terms as "energy transversion," "energy determinants," "decision arrivation," and "K.G. calories of energy consumption" are becoming nearly as common as was the special jargon of psycho-analysis a few years ago. One eminent journalist describes "technocracy" and all that relates to it as the biggest news material since the war. Yet one of the most eminent of the technocrats thus outlines the new doctrine which all America discusses:

The political administrations of the social states of the past and present price systems arose out of the steady state of doing work. The mechanism of these political orders of a price system are, and were, the mechanics of a static system in which the element of change in the rate of energy transversion does not enter. All of our social institutions have arisen out of an historical background which is to the technologist a steady state or a static system. The percentage of error which was inherent in the decision arrivation of the past was tolerable because the administrators who were called upon to execute these decisions were dealing with a price system in which the social rate, or the rate of the whole social mechanism, was unchanged from one period to another.

The process of decision arrivation used in a modern power-transmission system is without precedent or historical ancestors. The method of arriving at social decisions in a dynamic, continent-wide mechanism, wherein the element of change intrudes itself into every national rate of flow of goods or services, must be such that the intolerance or precision must be obtained in quantitative units peculiar to the rate which is being measured. It follows that this civilization on the North American continent must be operated on a thermo-dynamically balanced load.

Which somehow reminds one of what a cynical critic once said of a previous American religion: "If you would make a doctrine indestructible, make it completely incomprehensible. No one can then prove you wrong."

The plan, or doctrine, or cure, is certainly sweeping. It disposes of Communism as completely as it does of Capitalism. "Technological advancement in the past twelve years," writes another of the high priests of the new creed, "has definitely shattered all old social theory from that of the ancient Greeks through Karl Marx up to Veblen. It is unfortunate that most of our present economists are still floundering around with theories that have become mere folk-lore in the last decade."

Our present system, it tells us, is "fit only for the same museum in which are housed the pathetically inadequate political and economic theories of Plato, Marx and the great host of other diagnosticians and prophets who could not conceive of such a highly industrialized society as that in which we find ourselves to-day. Fascism, Communism and Socialism are likewise wholly inadequate to cope with our problem."

And if the new credo disposes of existing economic theories, it disposes just as airily of the future of Asia, Russia and England, which last the technocrats tell us "will soon be compelled to make a free gift of its surplus 35,000,000 population to its various colonial possessions."

As to Russia, a high priest of the new cult assures us:

Russia, in its Parthian retreat from Capitalism, has scored but a pyrrhic victory. It mistook the name-tag of a phase of the system for its entirety. It left the tag and took its essential mechanics. A social approach based upon the substitution of Hegelian dialectic for an Aristotelean dialectic may be an interesting intellectual pastime but of no functional importance, an example of the recrudescence of philosophic futility of European tradition.

As to England:

Among the futile gestures which probably will be made will be the complete abandonment of monetary currency and current banking credit, and stringent preferential tariffs and purchasing agreements to lessen the disparity which exists in its international balance of world trade. The United Kingdom, once the proud ruler of the seas and the unquestioned centre of the world's civilization, is fast disappearing from the scene and is helpless in the face of dissipated energy resources and technology.

Italy is in just as bad a situation. Of "the other nations and continents" we are told "little needs to be said":

Asia is hopeless as far as a high energy civilization is concerned. There aren't the resources available. Energy resources cannot be drawn out of words. You can't take more coal out of the ground than is actually there. Australia has very few resources. It has almost no opportunity for further development. South America is greatly lacking in many essential resources. Japan has attempted to operate a highly mechanized society under great handicaps. With limited resources and a high population density, she is reaching out to Manchuria, but there is little there to help her.

America alone may face the future secure. Again in the words of the high priest:

It is the only continental area of the world's surface manned, equipped and ready to move civilization into the new era where man for the first time in his progression from the jungle is the conqueror in the battle for leisure.

I have made these quotations not at all for purposes of derision—the way out may be along the road of technocracy for all I know, though curiously enough the technocrats do not tell us very precisely what that road is—but for the purpose of calling attention to the need of one technology which usually seems to be overlooked: a technology which will enable the layman to judge between one plan and another. For, as we have seen, however good a plan may be, one indispensable condition of its workability is that there shall be a sufficiently general agreement to adopt it; that it shall not be opposed by widely supported rival and mutually exclusive plans. The problem is not merely, or even mainly, to find out what is abstractly best. (To adapt a hackneyed analogy, whether the rule of the road is to go right or left matters less than that all should do the same.) The problem is to find that plan which will receive an acceptance general enough to ensure its smooth working, and which consequently will not challenge too violently established ways of thought and habit. Which means that any workable scheme must usually be a compromise between what is abstractly best and what, giving existing prejudices and habits, a confusedly thinking and intellectually conservative public will recognize as good. Which explains what a very good judge of the public mind meant when he said: The best plan is usually the worst.

And yet this is a truth which the Reformer type of mind seems particularly unwilling to admit. However new the plan of the Technocrats may be, its advocates reveal, as the quotations above made show, one quality which is very old indeed: a cocksureness, not merely that their own cure or treatment is effective, but that all other remedies are of no avail—ineffective, futile, poisonous, fatal.

Again, that may be true in an absolute and final sense. But unfortunately the same belief—that there is but one cure and that it forbids the application of any other whatsoever—is held by the adherents of other creeds of their remedy just as genuinely and sincerely; by the Communists of Marxism; by Single Taxers of Single Tax;

by Empire Free Traders of Empire Protection;
by many different schools of Currency Reformers
of their particular brand of currency reform.

And this very sincerity of the belief of each in
the exclusive virtue of his own remedy is the thing
which makes the application of any impossible.

This difficulty is made the more evident when
we remember that even when the specialists and
technicians are agreed, it is often impossible to
get their agreed recommendations applied by the
general lay public if those recommendations
happen to run counter to familiar conceptions
or to prejudice. How much more difficult, therefore, must be that necessary lay acceptance when
the specialists do not agree.

The authors of technocracy are engineers. But
as Mr. Walter Lippman has pointed out, the
engineer is not king in our economy. Democracy
is king—or has the right of veto.

In our social order the power is widely distributed among the
people, and it is their opinion, their prejudices, their notions of
their needs, and their interests which command us at all the
important moments of decision.

But the democracy, tho' it is king, is itself a limited monarch.
Its power is confined within the boundaries of the nation. Beyond
those boundaries it exercises influence, but not sovereignty.
Yet the affairs with which we have to deal, the plans we have to
formulate, the policies we adopt, are inextricably involved in a
world-wide economy.

Therefore, the attempt to abolish poverty and insecurity is
an engineering problem complicated by democracy and internationalism.

Inevitably it follows, I think, that the planning of a better
industrial order is the easiest and the smallest part of our task.

The difficult part is not in the domain of the engineer, but in the domain of the statesman and educator. It consists in finding plans that can be made acceptable to the democracy, and of adjusting harmoniously the separate plans and policies of some fifty sovereign nations.

I think the most apposite phrase I have seen in connection with the plans of the technocrats is that of Mr. George Soule, the American writer, who says that the technocrats have not really faced "the most difficult engineering job of all— the engineering of human consent."
Mr. Soule asks:[1]

Who is going to bestow power on the engineers? It is obvious that they haven't got it now. In spite of their scorn for Communists and Socialists, the Technocrats are really tagging after them, because both Communists and Socialists have worked out a technique for getting the power to do the sort of thing the Technocrats imply is necessary. I am not satisfied that either of these techniques is going to be successful, but at least the radical parties have not turned a blind eye upon the most difficult engineering job of all—the engineering of human consent.

There is, of course, something to be said, in a period of agitation, for concentrating on what is wrong and what you intend to do about it rather than upon the struggle to get the power to do anything. The Technocrats, like most advocates of economic planning, are helping to change people's ideas so that they will be more ready to support new political forms and powers. They serve a function in the large complex of social change. But in so far as they lead people to think that it is not necessary to do anything in politics or otherwise, that the change will come of itself and that we can just leave everything to Technocracy, they are telling a new kind of bedtime story to give children pleasant dreams while the house is burning down.

[1] *The New Republic*, December 28, 1932.

One incidental service of the technocrats will be to reveal the inadequacy of the conception of our problem as a mere clash between two rival classes for the possession of the means of production—a small minority of Capitalists or Bourgeois as against a massed proletarian.

The main theme of technocracy is that the productivity of the machine is so monstrous that there are no sufficient tasks left for man, and he does not know how to find means of consuming what he makes. The waste of war, or preparation for it by navy building, say, is in this situation a great economic relief; it helps us to dispose of our product and to keep men at work. Then the amount of goods consumed by a small idle class of bondholders would simply be no burden at all—if indeed a consuming class that is *not* working is not in terms of this theory a distinct blessing. To buy out the Capitalist by offering secure fixed interest bonds in return for their very insecure equities (creating thus consumption but not production and so easing over-production) on terms which would constitute for Capitalists a bargain which as business people they could not refuse, would seem a far more effective way of making the transition than revolution and all its dislocations and uncertainties could possibly be.

What, in the last analysis, is the *kind* of problem which confronts us in our major economic difficulties? How for instance, does unemployment arise? Voluminous and learned books have been written in answer to the question; yet in its fundamentals it is relatively simple.

Unemployment is a result of badly co-ordinated division of labour. A family on a primitive peasant farm, deriving everything they need directly from the soil, never know unemployment in our sense at all. The weather may prevent them from working, the drought render their work fruitless. But the absurdity of starving because they have produced too much never arises. And it never arises because the producer is also the consumer; the employer the employed; the seller the buyer, which means that the necessary co-ordinations are completely within control. When, however, a village arises, and one of the peasants becomes a blacksmith, no longer growing his own food, but depending upon getting it in exchange for bill-hooks or hoes which he makes, then *he* may well face unemployment. If the peasants have all the hoes they need, he will offer hoes in vain in exchange for potatoes, and may well starve in the midst of plenty.

In that situation two courses, broadly, are open to him. He may go back to being a peasant, growing his own food and making his own tools. It will mean a low standard of life; the peasants are no longer having their tools made by a specialist. But, at that standard, it will be a more secure life. Or he may remain a blacksmith, but adjust his activities more expertly, make something other than hoes which the peasants do want, and for which they *will* give food. But if he goes on with these elaborations he will soon find the co-ordinations passing altogether outside his control. He will arrive at a point where he is making machinery in a factory for some distant country, where some war or revolution or drought or bank failure may ruin his business. He has improved his standard of life; he is perhaps rich. But he is at the mercy of events on the other side of the world which he cannot control as he could control things while a simple peasant.

And that allegory represents broadly the alternative remedies before us: to go forward to still higher standards of life—to making, that is, the standards which have heretofore been the standard of a few the standards of all—which will mean increasing control over ever-increasing complexities; or to go back to less efficient production which will be more easily controlled but which will give lower standards of life.

The latter course is apt to be the more popular of the two. The Protectionist, finding that the natural advantage of some foreign country makes it possible for that country to produce some commodity more cheaply than it can be done here, and faced with the adjustment involved in withdrawing from that form of production and going into another, prefers instead to sacrifice the advantage which the natural foreign cheapness gives him. Trade Union resistance to labour-saving machinery is of the same general nature. And both may be successful in avoiding unemployment—at the cost of a general lowering of standards. Apply the method with complete thoroughness and you will get a complete cure for unemployment. Pass a law forbidding absolutely the importation into this country of anything whatsoever, and you will cure unemployment at one blow, for we should have to set every available man, woman and child to some form of labour (as we did during the war) in order not to starve to death. If a successful blockade, or some catastrophe of nature, actually achieved this end, there is no doubt whatever (in view of the war experience) that, faced by famine, we should find means of employing all available idle labour; and the unemployment problem would be solved. But our people would face a coolie standard of life. Which means that our problem is not to cure unemployment, but to cure unemployment without reducing, or sensibly reducing, the standard of life.

It is not a mere coincidence, but in the very nature of the case, that countries of very high standards of life should show a high unemployment figure, and countries of low standards of life a low one. Countries of the lowest standard— agricultural China, India—have relatively little unemployment in our sense. One statistician, who more than any other man in England, perhaps, has studied this question, said recently: "If I were to venture an over-simplified and over-sweeping generalization from my studies it might be something like this: As things are in the present system you can have high *per capita* productivity, wealth for the community, and unemployment. Or you can have low productivity and low unemployment; you cannot have great wealth, high productivity and no unemployment."

A modern motor-car is more efficient than the rude carts which preceded it; but it requires greater special mechanical knowledge to run it and keep it in running order. "The economic apparatus" of the peasant farm, or the mediaeval manor had a low standard of productivity; but it was easy to run; it was uncomplicated by the money device; the necessary adjustments by which all were kept at work were well within the control of the community concerned. It was because these adjustments—of production to consumption, and consumption to production, of time available, to jobs that needed doing; of the special capacity of this or that individual to this or that special task—were so much more controllable than with us that, though the tools were primitive, human industry never met the paradox so familiar to us that the more we (the community, which is now the world) produce the more risk do we run of utter poverty and ruin.

If the high productivity of our community is to be as well adapted to our needs as was the low productivity of peasant family to theirs, then we must learn to apply to the work of our national family of 1933 the kind of control and adjustment (though necessarily so much more complicated) that the self-sufficient manor applied to theirs:

we, too, must manage somehow to adjust in far greater measure than we do production to consumption, so organized as to make more efficiently the contacts of buyer and seller; guide more successfully than we do the man for the job and the job for the man; distribute our energies in the order of vital national need. *Laisser faire*—again we are generally agreed—does not do it. Yet every attempt to introduce co-ordination by means of governmental machinery is bitterly resisted by the most powerful forces of the business and industrial world, who immediately return to the assumption that from the anarchy of unguided, undirected individual effort will somehow emerge a final economic harmony, and that the best plan is to have no plan; that while it is true that politically a community could not live without organization and planning, the worst crime economically is for the community consciously to organize itself.

The average business man is obliged, of course, to admit that the very march of invention compels regulation: When transport was by horses and carts it could be an affair of unregulated individual enterprise upon which the community had no need to impose regulation. But when railways came, their very right of existence, their franchise, became, from the start, a matter of national regulation, even to price fixing. Activities like banking have followed the same drift from being, at the first, private, individualist, uncontrolled, to become public, collective, national, controlled. But only so far as business is pushed by absolute necessity will it accept this principle, and while admitting the utter breakdown of *laisser faire*, still shouts: "No governmental interference; no bureaucratic control: leave us alone."

The truth is that we funk—as well we may— the conclusion which results from the breakdown of *laisser aller* or of *laisser faire*. For the conclusion is that the logical alternative is a consciously directed and planned and controlled economy; and the complexity of the problem appals us. One recalls the efforts to make the necessary co-ordinations in one relatively small section of the industrial field, the Coal Industry: the years during which the obviousness of the chaos and the need of unification shouted aloud, but in vain, for remedy: the resistance to any real reform, the difficulty of even partial legislative action, the opposition, friction, sabotage —and then one thinks of what it would mean to multiply that a hundredfold or more. It is easy enough, it may be objected, to say: "Plan or Perish," and to talk of national planning for our national estate; but the task of centralized regulation and control of all the complex factors involved in modern industry is, we feel, so appallingly vast and difficult as to be beyond the administrative competence of any Government or economic community the world has yet known; to say nothing of the fact that much of it is an international problem. Remembering what governments, parliaments and bureaucracies are

where matters of practical business management
are concerned, is it any wonder, we may ask,
that the business world resists any invasion of
its province by those powers, and, while admitting
the failure of *laisser faire*, shrinks from its alternative and turns back to the old way?

To which the reply is, first, that a centralized
direction and co-ordination no more necessarily
involves interference in all the complexities of
our national industry than the existence of Central
Banks exercising a great deal of control necessi-
tates interference in all the complexities of banking
technique as worked by the constituent branch
or member banks; secondly, that one of the
characteristic tendencies (qualified it is true by
strong resistances) within the business world
itself is towards unified direction and control over
ever-widening areas—regional amalgamations,
with virtual price-fixing and market rationing
arrangements, tending to extend to international
cartels, so that the technique of the thing is being
developed outside governments, parliaments or
bureaucracies; thirdly, that the forces which
tend towards amalgamation or unification of
each industry within itself fail—and must without
outside help fail indefinitely perhaps—when it
comes to the co-ordination of one industry or
trade with another, necessary for correcting the
maladjustments that produce unemployment.

Note how these conclusions bear on the present
politico-economic situation. The industrialists,
admitting that *laisser faire* has failed and must

be replaced by conscious direction, still refuse
to organize that direction in any wide and com-
prehensive way. This attitude is marked by a
strange oscillation between such slogans as "we
must all pull together" and "trust to individual
initiative; no governmental interference." Admitting the need in general for co-ordination, they
oppose any particular case. Witness the history
of the attempted co-ordinations in the coal
industry.

Particularly do they not want direction by a
Labour Government. We are thus confronted by
this dilemma: A government which by its principles is pledged to co-ordination and "national
planning" cannot secure a really hearty co-operation on the part of those whose activities it ought
to co-ordinate. A Conservative Government
with which industry and finance would be tem-
peramentally fitted to co-operate would oppose
even the principle of national co-ordination, and
would trust instead to mere wage reduction,
and to such ancient nostrums as Protectionism and
economic Imperialism. The result is deadlock
and impotence. A Conservative Government
which, if it has the will to duplicate for peace
problems the national planning of war-time,
might secure from industry the necessary co-
operation, has not the will. A Labour Government which has the will is faced by the suspicion
and hostility of industry and business, ill-disposed
to put its back into the task of national co-ordination as it did during the war, and employing

betimes a subtle sabotage. "It's no good while the Socialists are in power. If we made a little profit, they would confiscate it. Carry on until they have gone and then we'll see what can be done."

What is the way out?

If indeed it is true, as it certainly is, that *laisser faire* having broken down, there must be organized control, conscious co-ordination; and if it is true, as it is, that the co-ordination cannot be by compulsion but must be by co-operation, we have somehow to find the basis of a Socialist-Capitalist co-operation.

The proposition that such a basis of co-operation can be found is not inconsistent with the belief that there is a real opposition of interest between worker and capitalist. We can accept the premise that Socialism is pledged to the replacement of the present order, and also agree that up to a given point there is a common interest. The two policies of "Socialism" and "Capitalism" are not in water-tight compartments: Capitalism is being compelled by the sheer irresistible drift of things to adopt more and more of Socialism —of public control, of ever-widening co-ordinations. At present it resists this tendency, accepts it sulkily with resentment. But it is here suggested that there is a wide field—to be indicated more precisely presently—in which an extension of Socialism, in the sense of co-ordination and control, would be accepted by British industry but for the forces just described which militate against acceptance.

Given, then, the presupposition that Labour is prepared to carry its policy into effect by increasing the amount of public control over a machine which it is its object to keep running smoothly and render increasingly effective, and that industry realizes that the choice is not between retaining the old *laisser faire* and Communism, but between utter chaos and collapse, and an orderly transformation into a new social system in which the technician, expert or business man will have his worthy place—given this, what should be the approach of a Socialist Government to securing that better control and national co-ordination?

The essence of the trouble, as we have seen, is certain maladjustments and disequilibria: the maladjustment of production to consumption and vice versa, of the number of miners available to the amount of coal needed and mined under rationalized methods which demand fewer men. Or there is a time lag in the investment of savings made by the rationalization, in industries which might employ the displaced men; a lag occasioned partly by the fact that people are slow to change habits and avail themselves of new devices like electrical equipment; partly also by the fact that men are slow to move from one occupation to another; partly because the long-term rate of interest does not fall as rapidly as the short-term rate.

The old automatic adjustments no longer suffice; there must be conscious adjustment, with ramifications so far-reaching that only a central authority could be entrusted with it.

Take a concrete example. It was foreseeable twenty years ago that the development of water-power, the coming of the internal combustion engine, the enormous push given to oil fuel, the development of foreign coal-fields, would greatly diminish the demand for British coal. Anyone watching tendencies could have said that there would shortly be half a million miners, perhaps more, too many. It was a problem against which some provision at least should have been made. Who's business was it to make it? Under the present system, nobody's. It was not the mining industry's. The business of the mining industry is to mine and sell coal. But though it is not the industry's business to tackle a problem of that kind, it would certainly have no objection to a Government tackling it. And had a Socialist or Socialized Government been in power at that time, it might, under the advice of its Board of National Economy, which by its study of the trend of markets and inventions had foreseen the contingency, have taken certain measures. It might have said: the next twenty years will in any case see the enormous extension of elec-trification; we will accelerate that development by a process of propaganda and education which will cause it to take place in five years, with appropriate propaganda among miners themselves to induce them to go into industries other than mining; we will establish training centres; we will accelerate all the research which might result in the discovery of means by which coal could be converted into oil; and by these methods, or a combination or adaptation of them all, we will "shock absorb" the change over from coal to oil and water-power.

Now the vantage-point from which the changes and developments just mentioned could best be perceived is from the vantage-point of the market. It has more than once been suggested that the point at which a Socialist-Capitalist co-operation —the co-operation, that is, of a Socialist Government with Capitalist organizations in possession or command of the machinery of production— could best be made is at the point of marketing. A Socialist Government, attempting to set up some sort of control and co-ordination of the nation's industries, might start mainly at the point of marketing: the rationalization of the nation's markets. That is at once the point of least resistance and the point of greatest strategic power. In saying to the nation's industries: "We are going to help you sell your goods," it would appeal to the least common denominator of motives. The motive which is common to every industrialist is the desire to sell his goods. But if the government had developed a technique by which, owing to the fact that its organization and marketing had made it in some sense an agent, in a position to bring large orders to a given industry, it would, of course, have power over that industry, be also in a position to bargain with it, to make conditions.

A government which has co-ordinated the

nation's markets has gone far to co-ordinate the nation's production and consumption, and to adjust the one to the other; to make those contacts the failure of which are the essential cause of unemployment.

How far and how quickly control is established will depend mainly upon two factors, concerning which certain things are to be noted.

(1) The spirit in which industry enters into co-operation with a government pledged to "national planning" of the war kind, if not of the war degree. If a Labour *movement* creates the impression that its objective is less the solution of unemployment than the smashing of Capitalism, and "chance what may come of the smash," it will be extremely difficult for a Labour *Government* to operate and extend control over industry.

(2) Much will depend upon where the government begins: whether the wedge enters at the thick or the thin end. Bulk purchase, Import Boards, quotas, are certain to come (they will be the only effective means of meeting a Russian export trade into which "cost of production," in the ordinary commercial sense, does not enter). But the attempt to begin with them might well delay their coming a quarter of a century.

How to begin control and where is of the essence of the problem. Once properly begun— begun, that is, with a real intention of success on the part of Industrialists and business men— control and co-ordination would grow of its own momentum. Begin at a point where it enlists the hostility of the business world, or in such a way as to provoke that hostility, and it is doomed to failure from the start.

I have described in some detail elsewhere the way in which such a "Home Marketing Board" might work. But whether that particular plan is feasible or not I suggest that the first National plan of all must be based upon the discovery of the ground upon which there may be provisional co-operation between the Socialist who desires to change the present order and the Capitalist who desires to change it; for in fact the Capitalist who opposes any change whatever in the present order is non-existent. The very growth of technique compels change. A year or two since a large employer of labour, an industrialist of the younger generation—and the better type—wrote to a member of the Labour Party thus:

Looking back over the last ten years and taking stock of my feelings as to what ought to have been done as various crises have arisen, I find myself much more of a Socialist than even the Left group of your fellows, if by Socialism you mean the pushing through by all forces in your power of a reconstructed social and economic order, without a general smash-up. Since the war we have had a good many serious industrial conflicts in which sometimes the whole industry of the country has been all but paralysed. But those terrific struggles have never been concerned with promoting any principle of social reconstruction: they have been precipitated by differences, sometimes small differences, over hours and wages; and when, after utter exhaustion, victory is achieved by your side, the general working of the system has not been rendered one whit more favourable than it was before; and not infrequently, in the inflationary period, a nominal victory was turned into an actual defeat by the fact that a rise in the price-level reduced the real value of the same nominal wages.

If your fight had been on the assumption that you desire the present system to remain unaltered, that it could perfectly well deliver what you want, the strategy might be sound. Even at that, however, you have allowed yourself to be drawn into a form of strategy which involves the engagement of your whole forces, and often nearly your whole available resources, on behalf first of one limited group, then the whole engaged again on behalf of another limited group. That method is bound sooner or later to result in exhaustion without any general advance, even of wage rates.

The contrast so often made, of the way in which we handled ammunition during the war, and the housing problem during peace, illustrates my point. There is no reason in nature, no difficulty that is of raw material or natural shortage, why we should not have handled housing in the big, sweeping national way that we handled ammunition.

He went on to describe the history of the "Weir" house and certain modifications of that plan which certain of his friends tried to get accepted.

It was not perfect; it could have been improved. (The cheap motor-car was not born perfected at the first attempt.) But, plainly, here we were working along the right lines, the right methods. The Labour Movement immediately began to rampage against those methods. It was at bottom, of course, a sectional fight. One section of Trade Unionism fearing that its field might be captured by another section; the fact being that, if the thing had developed, as it might have developed, the field of both would have been enormously enlarged.

I am familiar with that sort of outlook among my Capitalist colleagues, and have raged against it all my life. Why does Labour copy the worst side of Capitalist conservatism? The same thing was illustrated in the violent row about "dilution" in the building industry. Plainly, the tactic there, from the point of view of the permanent interest of Labour, was, not to fight against dilution, but to fight for guaranteed employment over long periods; and if costs could have been brought down in some such way as I have been suggesting, it would have been worth while for the employer, whether private or public, to give that guarantee.

He insisted that there was no general stand by Labour for the big "national plan"; there *was* an extremely obstinate stand for the protection of sectional interest; a method of protecting those interests, not by trading the old position for a better new one, but by insisting that the old position should, at all costs, be maintained.

This general attitude is carried over into discussions of such things as the unifying of building regulations throughout the country; one sectional interest is perpetually colliding with another. It is a strange fact that Labour will forget its sectional differences to protect purely sectional interests if those interests take the form of a wage or hours claim; it will not forget those differences in order to make a general advance in reconstruction.

I have listened many, many times to Socialist oratory about "the Capitalist" and his wicked plots; learning from these orators, as I sat there, just what my motives, my objects, my plans and crimes were—for I, as much as anybody perhaps, am "the" Capitalist. But however ignorant I may be of certain subtle points of the Marxian doctrine, there is just one subject in the world upon which I happen to be better informed than those orators are: that subject is my own plans, objects, motives. And on that subject, upon which, in the nature of things, I must know more than they do, they talk, if you will allow me to say so, the most piteous fustian and blatherskite. What they are searching for evidently is an outlet for emotion. Not to be able to indulge this invective and passion would, I have a feeling, deprive them of something which gives a certain intensity to their lives. Take away this fierce emotionalism and they would feel cold, starved, dull.

But the cost to their own movement of their emotional entertainment is a high one. It so twists strategy and policy as to stand in the way of co-operations which would be of immense service to the workers; it adds enormously to the resistances which Socialism has to encounter; and, in so far as Capitalism is, from the Socialist point of view, the enemy, it makes it impossible to destroy that enemy in detail.

For the assumption underlying this oratory I have referred to is that "Capitalism" in its interests is an entity, a single unit. Which, of course, is nonsense. One section of Capitalists or industrialists is often opposed in its interests to another; while the financier often finds himself set against the *entrepreneur*, the rentier against the user of money.

v

WHERE EDUCATION FALLS SHORT

It has not been the purpose of these lectures to
find some new way of escape, some new plan for
the restoration of prosperity, some new cure for
the depression. The purpose has been to find
why the public has not seen such ways of escape,
or such ways of avoiding some at least of the
evils from which we suffer, as have been indicated
by those competent to give the indication—has
not availed itself of the discoveries of the experts,
even when those experts are in complete agreement and when the reasons for the advice given
are almost self-evident. The lectures, in other
words, have been an inquiry into the reasons
which prevent the ordinary man from seeing the
simplest, the most fundamental of economic and
social truth.

Any such inquiry must prompt us to ask, of
course, how far education as now organized
for the millions is designed to help those millions
understand the world of which they will be a
part and as voters help to manage. One may ask
such a question without making, in any sense,
an "attack" upon our educational system or
indicting it in any way. Still less of criticizing
teachers, who perform, in many cases, marvels
of patience, and often achieve truly wonderful
results with a very defective tool, upon what is

sometimes very poor material. But I desire to remind you, as objectively and dispassionately as possible, of a few of the very simple facts which we have been considering.

The first is this: The management of the world, which went smash in 1914, was for the most part in the hands of highly educated people, belonging to classes which had possessed special advantages in that respect. Which meant that to be highly educated did not mean to be politically wise. One thinks of pre-war Germany. The school-master had been very much abroad in the land for the best part of a century before the catastrophe; its universities had philosophized over history and politics for longer still; its bureaucracy was the most intensely schooled in the world. The conduct of the relationship of States, European diplomacy of the pre-war era, was in the hands of a highly educated, specially trained order. And to-day, alike in Germany and France, some of the most disturbing and disruptive of the movements which push Europe nearer to chaos, the violent nationalisms, the disruptive animosities, find their main impulse in the educated classes, in the universities and professions.

The second fact we should face is this: the worst disasters which have come upon us could have been avoided if the ordinary man had grasped the social meaning of extremely simple everyday things, of the facts he already knew; if education had developed in him the skill or habit of applying to social problems simple truths inherent or self-evident in common facts of daily life.

That there is indeed this inability to see the social meaning of exceedingly simple things, it is impossible to deny. We have examined a number of instances: The story of the Reparations problem in Europe; the Debt problem in America; the fact that for years millions of the ordinary public maintained mutually exclusive demands upon debtor nations; made childish claims for "money, but no goods," when an intelligent child could be made to see that exports furnish ultimately the only means of payment.

And please do not dismiss the subject with some such suggestion as that "our curricula are too crowded to include economics." The thing goes far deeper than the mere omission of economics from the curriculum. Indeed, for reasons which I will indicate in a moment, I am not at all sure that I want economics included in the curriculum: We did not manage in the West to secure lay co-operation in the sanitary measures urged by medical experts through teaching bacteriology in the school. The seriousness of the thing arises from the fact, not that it indicates failure to understand economics, but that it indicates failure in the understanding of our own nature and its relation to society, a whole range of simple social phenomena the comprehension of which is indispensable to the management of the world in which we live. If the Reparations muddle as an instance of the failure of the

public to understand a very simple condition
of good economic health stood by itself, it
would still be significant. But it does not stand
by itself. It is a type of error which charac-
terizes and explains a fundamentally defective
and distorting way of thought in the public
mind, which so long as it is uncorrected must
condemn our democratic societies to disastrous
strains and dislocations, and make it impossible
for any cure which we may apply to work effectively. The instance itself is significant both
because the failure to see this simple point really
did obstruct the economic and financial restoration which all were praying for; and because none
of the great financial interests were opposing
settlement. You did not have, as you have,
perhaps, in the case of armaments and war, great
vested interests throwing their influence on the
side of disorder and conflict. None of the great
interests of Capitalism profited from the prolongation of the chaos which the failure to settle Reparations involved. The great financiers, after the
epilepsy of war had subsided a little, were in
favour of the step which has at last been taken,
just as the bankers in America to-day are in favour
of cancellation or reasonable adjustment. There
is no plot of Capitalism or Imperialism involved
in this. Furthermore, the Socialists and Radicals
were from the first against Reparations, so that
in this matter you have had the bankers, the
leaders of labour, and the theoretical Socialists
all of one mind. What opposed them were not

informed minorities anywhere, but the great mass
of men and women, the "anonymous millions,"
the readers of Trust newspapers exploiting popular prejudice, the readers of the picture-papers,
the readers of the Hearst Press in America, the
tabloids; Mr. Babbitt or John Citizen the world
over; and that must include much of the rank
and file of the House of Commons, Chambers of
Commerce, Clergy, Trade Union members; in
other words, general lay opinion as distinct from
the views of those who have made some specialized
study of the subject. The experts on the one side,
the lay public on the other.

I say that, given the extreme simplicity of the
issues involved, this case of the Reparations and
Debts muddle would have been significant as an
instance of sheer confusion of thought on a public
concern of elementary simplicity. But it does not
stand alone. It typifies a general failure.

I am aware that in respect of much of the
foregoing criticism you will enter a caveat. You
will remind me that education is not merely or
mainly a matter of schooling, but of home life,
the life of the world and the influences which
play upon our minds through, say, the Press.
These, you may urge, are more powerful than
the school. That may well be true; to the extent
that it is, it merely supports the plea that in so
far as it is possible to give the young mind a start
in the right direction and with right habits, it
should be done. But one has to add something

more. The public gets the Press and the popular literature it deserves; editors give the public what it wants. Many successful editors and newspaper proprietors, for instance, evidently assess the education of the public at some such standard as this: It has not learnt the multiplication table; one row of noughts means to it the same thing as any other row of noughts.

This is not mere rhetorical extravagance. Take the point I have referred to before in these lectures—the newspaper rampage about the cost of the League. I take the instance because here is something that can be subjected to definite, measurable, ponderable test. The campaign has gone on now for several years: none of the papers loses caste or prestige by it, and I think the campaign has had the effect of persuading tens of millions of Englishmen that the cost of the League to us constitutes a serious drain upon our national resources. Yet the size of the burden, like the weight of the argument, is capable of exact measurement by a sum in arithmetic which any reader could presumably do in sixty seconds. Our national income is about thirty-three hundred million sterling, and was recently rather more; our contribution to the League a little over a hundred and fifty thousand. That is to say, that contribution bears the same relation to our national income that a contribution of something less than three shillings a year would to a man with an income of considerably over three thousand pounds. And the three shillings

M

is designed to build up a substitute for a method of defence which has involved the three thousand a year man in an expenditure of about five hundred pounds a year. What should we say of a man with over three thousand a year who keeps on harping to his friends that a subscription of three shillings a year for membership in a club designed to make the neighbourhood he lived in less liable to ruinously costly lawlessness was more than he could possible afford? It is a simple statement of fact to say that if he harped on the point of this "extravagance" to the extent to which the *Daily Express*, the *Daily Mail*, the *Evening News*, the *Evening Standard*, and other papers continue to harp on the League "expense," we should, without any hesitation, say that he was nearing the point of certifiable lunacy.

The millions who read these papers may have "learnt" the multiplication table, but they have certainly not learned to apply it to daily judgments.

Take another aspect. At the time of the making of the Peace Treaties any criticism of their severity was sufficient to banish a politician from public life.

The terms of the Peace Treaties, explained, among other papers, the *Morning Post*, were not half severe enough. They were so lenient, indeed, explained the *Morning Post* (June 16, 1919), that:

. . . those who know Germany best fear that she will remain after these terms are imposed the strongest power on the Continent of Europe, and will soon again be in a position to threaten and bully her neighbours. In these circumstances the most valuable parts of the Treaty from our point of view are those parts which permanently curtail the material and industrial resources of Germany, upon which her military power is built. The transfer of Upper Silesia to Poland, of Alsace-Lorraine and the Saar Valley to France, are to our thinking not justice only but insurance against future trouble. For let us be certain that every atom of power which Germany retains she will use against us. Nothing we can do will reconcile her: our policy should, therefore, be directed to reducing her power. And any weakening of that policy endangers the security and peace of Europe and our own existence.

A year or two passes, and in the same *Morning Post* you get this:

The banking and currency systems of the world have broken down, and for the time being international co-operation, a necessity for their proper functioning, has almost ceased. . . .

To focus attention upon the unequal distribution of the world's gold is to see the symptom without appreciating the cause of the *débâcle. This is to be found in the economic clauses of the Peace Treaties and nowhere else. . . .*[1]

The Peace Treaties imposed upon Germany, and to a much smaller extent upon her former allies, the obligation to make large and continuous payments to the victorious Powers. Those payments could be made either in goods or in gold, and since the gold at the disposal of the paying countries was an insignificant amount compared with the extent of their obligations, it followed that they could fulfil these treaty obligations only by exporting vast quantities of goods to those countries which were entitled to reparations or indemnities.

But the last thing that the receiving countries desired was a continuous influx of foreign-made goods into their territories, and no sooner did the process of payment begin than they resorted to all sorts of devices to protect themselves from the dislocation

[1] My italics.

and injury which the newly created and artificial trade channels threatened to bring in their wake.

. . . To talk of restoring the gold standard while these conditions remain unaltered is to ignore fundamentals. . . . International action could do more in a few days to readjust the financial mechanism than the most earnest efforts of any single Power in as many years. . . .

When the Peace Treaties were under discussion nothing made the type of critic who is now rampaging against the League so angry as the suggestion that it was unwise—and unsafe—to create the new Europe in such a fashion that France would be so militarily preponderant that she could once more dominate Europe. To make such a suggestion was to "stab a faithful ally in the back," to accuse her of a militarism which everyone knew was the exclusive possession of Germans.

One calls Lord Rothermere's "Hats Off to France" in support of an outrageous invasion of German territory to enforce the payment of Reparations which practically everyone now proclaims to be mischievous and financially disastrous. Note the popular Press to-day.

The *Daily Express*, where international politics are dealt with by Viscount Castlerosse in the intervals of telling us what the dear Duchess told him in the Carlton, says (June 3rd):

The two factors which make war certain in Europe are the ever-increasing militarism of France and the Peace of Versailles which was a peace to end peace.

The attitude of the League of Nations towards these two points is reminiscent of the agitated posterior of an ostrich with its head firmly fixed in the mud.

At Geneva to-day the Dove of Peace is completely dominated by the Gallic cock.

Europe, to a great extent due to the weakness of the League of Nations, is seething, and Geneva is the cauldron now stuffed full of injustices and grievances which have nothing to do with us.

Remembering the "Hats Off to France" and similar manifestations of but a year or two since, one wonders whether the editors of these Jingo papers credit the public with any memory at all when they base their attacks upon the League largely on the allegation that it is the instrument of French policy. "A. A. B.," in the *Evening Standard*, writes:

France wants to keep Germany and the succession States poor so that she may dominate Europe as Germany did twenty years ago. It is curious how invariably a surplusage of gold ruins nations. The payments by the French after 1871 did Germany nothing but harm, as is now admitted.

The popularity of this line of identifying the League with French preponderance is evidenced by the fact that non-political papers of the pictures-of-actresses type join in the hue and cry. Thus a writer in the *Bystander:*

The League is intent on bolstering up and aiding by every means in its power the most militaristic nation in the world— France. France has the League in her pocket. People like Lord Cecil of Chelwood either cannot see this or see it and approve of it.

Yet anyone who reads the Press at all must know that the French Chauvinist is as bitterly

hostile to the League as is the Jingo in England.
The quotations just made could be duplicated
almost any day from the *Echo de Paris* ("Perti-
nax"), the *Petit Parisien*, the *Figaro*, and half a
dozen other papers. And he would note also that
the chief allegations against the League are that
it is worthless, because plainly Britain does not
intend to fulfil the obligations taken under its
Covenant; because it is "notoriously a mere
appanage of the British Foreign Office," "dominated by the Anglo-Saxons," and a trap for
placing France under the control of foreigners
and depriving her of her independence. Incidentally, the Chauvinist papers in France support
Japan as against China, as our Jingo papers do
here.

Certain of the weekly reviews join the dailies.
The *Saturday Review* concludes an article on the
Manchurian situation:

> The long and short of the matter is that Great Britain must set
> her face against all foreign entanglements. It is high time that
> our rulers realized that the interests of the Empire must come
> first; if these prove incompatible with membership of the League,
> then Great Britain must say farewell to Geneva. We are not
> going to alienate our old friend and ally Japan for the *beaux
> yeux* of Viscount Cecil and the League of Nations.

Repetition would be wearisome. But one suggestion put forward by the *Evening News* (of the
Rothermere group) deserves notice as bearing
upon the question of public forgetfulness. It
expresses the view that the methods which the
nations followed before the war were more

successful in preserving peace than those implicit in the League:

In the absence of the League the nations acted for themselves, and they acted promptly. In nine cases out of ten they acted to good effect. . . .

The League, all solemnity and gas, has no boots to kick with, and, worse still, no posterior to which the foot of urgency can be applied. The old personal method was better.

Well, this view of the editor of the *Evening News* and other editors, that the pre-war way was good enough and quite successful, prompts one to present a few reminders.

Practically every statesman of eminence connected with the beginnings of the war, every serious student of its genesis, has testified to the fact that the war was the outcome, the inevitable outcome, of the old diplomatic and political system of Europe. Asquith, Grey, Balfour, Bonar Law, Lloyd George, Baldwin, Ramsay MacDonald, Cecil, Henderson, among the English; Wilson, Taft, and (privately, and by the implication of recent acts) Hoover, among the Americans; have testified to the need of replacing the old method by one based on the principle of the League. (Lord Grey, the Minister in charge of Britain's foreign policy when this country entered the war, has said in effect that if there had been a League of Nations in existence in 1914 there would have been no war.) No one pretends now—as the papers above quoted used to pretend —that war was due to the special wickedness of Germans, the sudden swoop of a satanic wolf in a peaceful world lusting to eat such harmless lambs as France and Russia, and to take on at one and the same time a dozen other States. The war arose because the essence of the old system was that the defence of each nation was its own affair, and that the community of nations had no concern in seeing justice done to any member whose rights might be violated by a stronger. But reading the Press to-day one is prompted to doubt whether education has equipped us to apply even elementary arithmetic to problems of public policy; and still more whether education has given us any understanding of the nature of society. By the very laws of mathematics—since each of two parts cannot be the stronger—the old system was bound to break down as a means of defence. In practice it meant the formation of rival alliances based on this type of log-rolling: Nation A said to Nation B: "If you will let me have my way in my little difference with C, I will see that you have yours in your difference with D." It was known as maintaining the Balance of Power, and involved, of course, complete anarchy.

I ought not to leave the impression that the problem of the Press—itself a factor of education —is merely one of the school. It is not. The social problem of the big circulation popular newspaper is this: At just the time when, in order to prevent some act of egregious folly, it is necessary to remind the public of facts they like to forget, no ordinary daily paper fighting to preserve its circulation against the competition of popular rivals can afford to tell the unpopular truth, bring out the unpopular fact. It is better business, from the point of view of circulation, to confirm the public in its half-truths (or whole falsehoods) than to tell it what it does not want to hear.

To illustrate. When certain papers were exploiting the "corpse factory" rubbish during the war, I said to the editor of a certain popular newspaper: "Do you mean to tell me that you seriously believe this tripe?" To which he replied: "Of course I don't. But it's a first-class story, and if I don't splash it, Jones across the street will, and run off with my circulation. And I intend to run off with his before he can do it."

But that sort of thing, of course, explains the Treaty of Versailles. As the result of being fed during four years with fare of that kind, we came to the Peace Settlement hardly sane, not concerned really with the future effects of the Treaty upon our own permanent interests, or with the feasibility of Reparations: concerned only to hit back, to retaliate, to "punish." We took at that time a view of the German which nine hundred and ninety-nine out of a thousand of us would declare to-day to be wicked nonsense. Most of us would in all sincerity deny that we ever held the views we then so freely expressed.

It would have been hard enough at best to have held balanced views. It is not in human nature to be impartial in such circumstances.

It was entirely "natural" to want to hit back. But if we always did what is "natural," with no social discipline at all, no consideration of the ultimate consequences to ourselves of "obeying that impulse"—well, of course, there would never have been any civilization at all. Civilization is largely a process of substituting for the first thought, a second. It does not, fortunately, mean a denial of the life of impulse, because the second thought sets up another impulse often just as satisfactory to satisfy as that provoked by the first thought. There are Americans who "obey that impulse" to burn Negro girls and boys alive (there have been two lynchings down South this last ten days). But there are, fortunately, other Americans in whom a second thought has set up the impulse to declare that kind of thing a foul and detestable exhibition of savagery. To obey the impulse to wipe this blot from the American escutcheon will not probably prove less satisfying than the indulgence of the "human nature" which prompts the burning alive of men, women and children for no proved offence. The impulse resulting from the second thought would be much commoner than it is if Southern newspapers made their readers acquainted with the real facts of the lynching phenomenon. (Most Southerners, indeed most Americans, flatly deny the truth of even the undeniable statistics about lynching.) But what paper in the Black Belt, careful of its circulation among the Whites, would dare to emphasize the kind of fact which must be brought home to the White population if the impulse to wipe out this abomination is to be set up and maintained?

The Peace Treaty was, of course, a vast lynching party—characterized by all the elements which distinguish a lynching from an orderly trial. Indeed, most of the big decisions of modern democracy, as we know it, are characterized by most of the elements that distinguish a lynching from an orderly trial. If we are trying a case of theft, or even an ordinary civil case concerned with the question of a few pounds' worth of property, we take elaborate precautions to see that both sides of the case secure full, organized presentation; we hear the evidence by well-defined laws of evidence; we remove those who are to decide the question of guilt from the infection of group passion, partly by actual physical seclusion, partly by forbidding prejudgment of a case by the Press until evidence has been heard; but mainly by a tradition of respect for the principle that there *can* be no such thing as a fair judgment unless both sides have been heard, the side of the alleged criminal as well as the side of society. We make definite provision for the skilled and expert presentation of the alleged criminal's case, even though the alleged crime may be of the foulest; there must be no stretching of the laws of evidence against him, and guidance of the judge must scrupulously respect the rule that without the fullest hearing of both sides there can be no possibility of right judgment.

So much for the relatively simple—and relatively unimportant—matters of theft, disputes about property, responsibility for damage, and so forth. Long experience has proved to us that the plainest-looking case has two sides, and that because human evidence is so astonishingly unreliable, judgment so apt to be distorted by prejudice and irrelevance, the disciplines and techniques for hearing the two sides which we associate with disputes of the legal kind are absolutely indispensable.

But when we come to the much more vital questions of public policy—the settlement of Europe after a war which has cost ten million lives, mistakes in which may involve another war costing another ten million lives; economic or financial policies, tariffs, the gold standard, involving the property and welfare not of one person but of forty million, or four hundred million, then, for decision on these things the ultimate judge—which is the big public—shamelessly violates all the rules of evidence; the tradition then is not to hear both sides, but to regard the hearing of the other side as proof of treason, lack of patriotism, moral perversion. Every means of inflaming sheer passion and prejudgment, of obscuring the real issue by irrelevancies, is seized upon if such pandering is a proved means of increasing the value of those great industrial properties (in which many millions of pounds have been invested) that our modern "big circulations" have become.

The process may not be deliberate or intentional, but at certain stages of popular rampage it becomes inevitable. The paper which would state the Negro case, the German case—or, on the other side of the fence, the White case or the English case—would simply be dropped and so disappear, in favour of one where no such heresies were ever permitted. It is the Gresham Law of economics applied to public advocacy: the bad coin drives out the good.

When the late Lord Northcliffe bought *The Times*, he was very full of what a truly national paper ought to be. (In justice to his memory it may be recalled that before the war, which vitiated all values, it was a regular practice for the Northcliffe Press, notably the *Daily Mail*, to publish articles expressing a point of view diametrically opposed to the paper's own. I myself regularly contributed to the *Mail* "page four" articles, running at times to two columns, condemning the policy which Northcliffe was then following. His successors seem to be cast in different mould. One does not see the *Daily Express*, for instance, publishing the case for the League of Nations.) In conversation with Northcliffe one day I suggested—in a form somewhat along the lines of the case just stated—that no newspaper, unless it gave the facts much as a judge would insist upon the facts being wrung out in a difficult case, could profess to be a national one; that there was an all but irresistible tendency for a paper, in its competition for circulation, to exploit momentary prejudices to the exclusion of the whole truth; and I added that, even if he, Northcliffe, managed to make a really impartial paper successful, what about his successors after his death? He then unfolded a plan which was running in his mind at the time: to place *The Times* under a National Committee like that which is responsible for the British Museum, and put it up to them to see that the "get-the-facts-and-hear-all-sides policy" should be maintained.

The idea was never, of course, carried into effect. But when broadcasting reached a stage where legislation became necessary, this principle of giving impartially alike the facts and rival interpretations of them was established. The responsible authority of the B.B.C. was placed in something of the position of a judge. Not "what'll sell the paper" but "what ought the public to know in order to be in a position to judge both sides" and form sound judgments in moral, literary, social and political questions, became, in theory at least, the standard.

Let us hope that that standard has not been abandoned.

The principle involved is immeasurably more important than is generally realized, and only the public can decide what principle shall really prevail. If it has wisdom, it will say:

In the past we have at times gone grievously wrong on policy because the newspapers anxious for our custom have been concerned mainly to tell us what they think we should like to hear. But we want the facts upon which a sound judgment can be based, and we know that that will at times involve hearing things which run counter to our prejudices and conventional standards. Hearing both sides, as a jury would hear them, means a readiness to hear things which offend our prejudices, things which we regard as subversive, or it has no meaning at all. And that is just as true in the region of morals as in that of politics or sociology. It is a principle indispensable to the efficient working, indeed the safety, of that method of "government by discussion" of which we are supposed to be the inventors, and which we call democracy. We insist that the principle shall be respected and still further developed and organized, and not replaced by unstable personal standards like those which the more popular of our newspapers have heretofore maintained to our infinite cost in public sanity and wisdom.

But, to return once more to the problem of school education, more must be done in the school itself to make our millions aware that it is impossible to know the truth unless we are prepared to hear both sides; that there is a moral obligation upon all of us to be ready to do that. It is not an easy thing to do, an easy attitude of mind to maintain, and perhaps only early habit can make it possible at all. Yet without it we go to disaster.

There are certain commonplaces, touching what might be called the primary philosophy of daily life, that ought to be and could be of universal possession. Anyone who knows anything at all of the public mind, the voting mind, the mind which ultimately determines policy, knows that those necessary commonplaces of successful life in the modern world, far from being of universal possession, are of very rare possession.

Our education has usually completely failed to

leave any awareness of what on the one hand
human nature is really like, and on the other any
perception of the principles which must be applied
if any society is to work at all, of how man can be
fitted to society and society to man. It is doubtful
whether most of those who come out of our
schools are even aware that what they are supposed
to have been learning all those years is the nature
of man and the nature of society. In any case,
most of those who have been produced by our
education have not been able to distinguish
between the relationships or attitudes which are
anti-social, which make society completely unworkable, and those which do not.

If it be true that education has failed to develop
in the millions that pour through its mills the
particular skill or aptitude for discerning the
social meaning of the facts that stare us in the
face, if it is possible for the world to ignore again
and again in its behaviour the things which it
already knows, or might know quite easily, what
will it avail to give the new generation, through
our education, knowledge of more facts? It can
ignore the new knowledge as easily as it ignored
the old. Not fresh knowledge, but greater skill
in seeing the relevance to our problems of already
known fact, would seem to be one of the first
needs of a reformed education. Ignore this truth
and no erudition that you subsequently add, no
knowledge of history, of the quarrels of Balkan
States, of the facts of their ethnographic compo-
sition, of the lives of our statesmen and generals,

of the strategy they employed in their battles, can be of any help. Pile fact on fact, fact on fact, fact on fact till his life's end, and it will not provide the tiniest help in enabling their possessor to find the way of escape if the interpretation is twisted, if the compass of his ship has serious deviation. Until that deviation is corrected—until he can truly interpret what he already knows—it serves no purpose to provide him with further fuel for the stoking of the ship's engines. It may only make the smash all the greater when the error of the compass has piled the ship on the rocks.

Yet I have known deeply learned men try all their lives to steer their ship with a faulty compass—a grossly defective method of interpretation. My suggestion is, let us first of all get the compass right. It does not really dispose of the effects of the error to say that the remedy is "too simple."

If we do not get the elementary things straight at the start, learning cannot help us: it only results in carrying a heavier impedimenta along the wrong road, making the journey back on to the right road the more difficult. It is as though every detail—engines, machinery, stores, charts— in the equipment of a great ship about to embark upon reef-infested seas had been painfully worked out; but the compass forgotten, as too trivial a thing for the attention of the highly trained technicians employed.

We live in an age which positively reeks of

N

psychological jargon—of complexes, and fixations, and transferences, of complicated sexual explanations for the fact that you trip over the door-mat when you come in, or dreamt that the booking clerk would persist in giving you first class when you wanted third.

Yet people who can give you these complicated explanations (that sort of psychological reading is very difficult to avoid these days if you read even as much as the picture papers), full of bemusing and remote explanations of behaviour, are often, in their attitude to public policy, guilty of the type of elementary error in applying the plain facts of human nature to human society with which these lectures have dealt. I want in conclusion to recall the nature of these errors and the purpose of pointing them out.

A typical one, with which I have dealt at some length, concerns the relation of anti-social human impulse to human institutions: the "human nature" argument used so often as a reason for opposing international institutions; the argument which runs: Nations have moods of great irrationalism, pugnacity, vindictiveness; therefore we must be careful not to allow a League to be established nor to encourage the habit of international co-operation: motorists are apt to be such road hogs, therefore let us have no traffic rules. Millions of educated folk go their lives through with the "human nature" argument turned completely upside down, either because they have no realization of the fact that constitutions, laws, rules, restraints, Ten Commandments, exist *because* the nature of man is at points and at periods so anti-social or because their education has not given them the aptitude to apply a simple fundamental truth about human nature and human institutions to a slightly less familiar situation.

The general attitude which results from this bad philosophy has immediate and disastrous results in practical policy. Together with other fallacies as transparent, it deeply affects the success of efforts like the Disarmament Conference, failure of which will, in its turn, owing to the lack of confidence which failure would provoke, affect the economic settlement of the world. Just as we have had to have Conferences without number, and made pretences of settlements, which were no settlements, about Reparations, because the public, not being clear on the fundamental point, would not have it otherwise, so in the matter of Disarmament we have the same paralysis, and are likely to have it again repeated in the World Economic Conference.

You will note that I have attached great importance to what might be termed the fatalistic implication of the attitudes described; the way of thought in social and political matters it indicates. For just as it is an innate fatalism, mainly, which frustrates the efforts of the doctor in the East in dealing with pestilence, so, I believe, that it is an innate fatalism—the sense that we really cannot do anything about it—which in the West is mainly accountable for our failure to create an international society and deal collectively with our basic economic maladjustments.

But is not this habit of thought, buttressed as it is by crudely defective reading of everyday facts, something which it is the job of the educationalist to modify? Is it really impossible, by the way in which education deals with the events of history, the facts of the world, of our nature, of society, to bring home to students the essential fallacy of this fatalist tendency or interpretation, and to replace it by a sense of what man might do by the power of his intelligence and a sense of his obligation to apply it? We teach "facts" about life in other countries. Well, the fatalism of the East and some of its social and political results are a very important fact. What man has done by his institutions to change human behaviour is another, and might be related to the first. These facts are just as important as the correct dates of the deaths of kings or a knowledge of statistics of population. Furthermore, a realization of how far human behaviour has changed as the result of knowledge has an effect upon the mind entirely different from that produced by a knowledge of statistics and dates. Knowledge of how man's will or understanding has altered behaviour, and altered the world, helps to determine a moral attitude, a way of looking at life as a whole. A boy might know the exact population of every country in the world accurately, but the knowledge would have no such effect upon his moral outlook as the realization of the way in which institutions, laws, social organization, have made it possible for a tolerable civilization to be based on sometimes very defective human nature.

Another prevailing misconception with which I have dealt as a primary factor in the creation of economic fallacies and international conflict is the deeply ingrained tendency of the human mind to confuse symbols with the things they represent; of the way in which we symbolize a nation as a person—"Uncle Sam," "John Bull" —and then in our minds make the symbol a thing of actual flesh and blood, a person, to be hated as an enemy, supported as an ally, or feared as a trading competitor; although in fact, even as an economic entity, the thing is largely figment and the source of disastrous economic mistakes. This tendency to personify abstractions is, it is true, a "natural" tendency. But for just that reason surely the business of education is to create in the minds of those apt to tumble into these pitfalls an awareness of their presence, to give the skill which will enable the ordinary man, by being on the alert, to avoid them.

I find it suggestive, by the way, that I am so often accused of over-simplification, of making our problems more simple than in fact they are, by critics who insist upon treating nations as persons. What over-simplification could be grosser, more misleading, more mischievous than that which causes us habitually to talk about nations as a single entity; which led us at the

Peace to divide the world into "good" nations
and "bad" nations; which leads men of letters
like Mr. Kipling to tell us, in this year of grace
1933, that "the" Boche is as evil as ever and has
learned nothing since the war?

I am suggesting to you that it is the failure to
grasp points as simple as that there is no such
thing as "the" Boche, but sixty-five million
separate and distinct Boches, that Germany is
not one person—things as elementary as this
which make us miss the road in public policy,
miss the way of escape.

A closely related problem which we touched
upon was the fact that our electorates have plainly
not been taught the trick—not an easy one to
learn—of asking themselves clearly what government and politics are for, what they really want
of organized society.

During most of the time that men are exercising their political functions, casting their votes,
writing their political programmes, clamouring
for this or that policy, they quite plainly have not
settled in their minds what it is they want. Ask a
voter what he is voting for, and he will rationalize
to the extent of declaring that he wants welfare.
But ask an astute electioneer what makes electors
vote for a given candidate, and he will give you
indubitable evidence of the fact that what the
voter wants is his emotions fed, his animosities
pandered to. The candidate who in the election
of 1918 dealt at all dispassionately with the
probably injurious effects of large indemnity

claims upon British welfare was all but invariably
rejected in favour of the candidate who filled his
speeches with plentiful references to German
wickedness and the need for punishment. The
voter might have said that he wanted to secure
the peace and the prosperity of his country.
But an intelligent child could have seen that the
kind of peace for which he was clamouring would
have been fatal to those ends—as indeed many
of the voters who shared in the clamour are now
declaring. The voter's educational preparation for
his task had not resulted in making him aware of
his own nature or capable of weighing one want
against another, or indeed of discerning what
his real wants were. And one's mind goes back
to such political events as the Dreyfus case; the
mystic militarism of pre-war Prussia; the long
years when Anglophobia in America was a powerful electoral factor; to Mayor Thompson of
Chicago, and asks whether the millions who were
swayed by the motives which marked those inci-
dents had really been taught to discern the object
of politics and government, of our laboriously
created society.

Education has not enabled the mass of men to
apply to public policy, the gravest of public acts,
the most fundamental of all questions: What do
I want? What is my purpose in following this
course?

The tragic proof lies in our attitude to-day
towards the things for which we were supposed
to have waged the war. Why did the nations fight

in 1914? What did they want? What did they fear? There were certain answers: They wanted economic opportunities. Freedom. No Prussian regimentation. To make the world safe for Democracy. But after the war those who had been fighting for freedom or democracy treated those things with the utmost contempt. While it is certain we were actuated by ambitions, fears, vengeance, hatreds, what is equally obvious is that we had not asked ourselves: Ambitions, to what end? Fear of what? Vengeance against whom? We feared the enemy's victory. But what did we fear he would do to our disadvantage? The French desired to avenge past injuries, but had not asked whether the vengeance would be upon those responsible for the injuries. We wanted power, but did not know how we should use the power.

The most certain thing of all to-day about the war is that no one is quite clear what he was fighting for; what he was fearing.

The degree to which education has left on the mind of the millions a comprehension of the nature of society may be gathered from another fact to which we have devoted some attention: the all but universal acceptance of, and belief in, anarchy as a method of living together in the modern world; the belief that in this closely packed world we do not need any organized society at all. You stare, because you don't realize in what sense men believe in anarchy. We do, it is true, believe in an organized society so far as the life of individuals within

each State is concerned; we recognize that in
our closely packed populations of train-catching,
and sewage disposal, and crowded roads, there
must be rules; but we believe that in the relationship of States this principle can be completely
reversed and that the true way of international life
is to have no government. Why do we suppose
anarchy will answer in the international field
when we know it will not as between individuals?
Put that question to the ordinary man, and if he
is honest he will admit ninety-nine times out of
a hundred that he has never thought it out,
that the contrast has never occurred to him. I
suggest that if his education had taught him to
think about society at all, the contrast would have
disturbed him very much indeed. For the war
came, as the next war may come, not because
men are wicked, still less because one particular
nation is much more wicked than any other,
but because the nations as a whole, in constant
and daily contact, with the views of one nation
as to its rights in conflict with the views of another
as to those rights, facing all the familiar difficulties
of the human community, refused to create
common rules of conduct and institutions for
their enforcement—refused, that is, to apply to
international relations the commonest, the most
universal, the most conclusive human experience.

The commonest daily experience teaches us
that if each is to be, in his relations with another,
judge of his own rights—which means being
judge of the rights of that other as well—there

must be conflict. For each is demanding a right
which he denies the other. Equally must there be
conflict if each, in order to be secure, demands
to be stronger than the other: arithmetic inter-
venes. These are the familiar paradoxes of social
anarchy, which no sane person would think of
urging as a workable method in closely packed
civilized communities. And of war—so nearly
related in its effects, and probably in its causes,
to the present disintegration of our society—one
can say this: It may have many causes, it may have
one, which may be unknown, but this much is
certain: it will inevitably arise so long as we have
international anarchy. The abolition of anarchy
may not cure war, but its presence will inevitably
cause it.

Yet the net result of our education, of all our
history teaching, our academic philosophizing,
was a practically universal belief in or acceptance
of anarchy as the normal condition in international relationship. Educated men everywhere
accepted the international anarchy as the natural
relationship of States; strenuously defended it,
passionately resisted projects which would modify
it. Let us be frank as to the nature of that acceptance. The public as a whole did not say: "Of
course, the absence of international institutions,
the method by which each is his own defender
must end in conflict, but we accept war as the
price we pay for certain other advantages attaching
to national sovereignty and independence." They
said in effect: "War need not arise from this

situation if other nations behave as well as we do. War does not inhere in this particular system; it is the result of the misbehaviour of foreigners." That is not merely what most of the educated world said before 1914; it is what most of the educated world says to-day. Certainly the ordinary man does not see in the demand for the maintenance of peace and of national sovereignty a contradiction of the principles upon which all organized society is founded. He does not see the contradiction because he has not been made familiar through his education with the necessary mechanism of society (as he has been made familiar, for instance, with the fundamental mechanism of the heavenly bodies, the rotundity of the earth, the law of gravity, and so forth) and he has not had developed in him the habit of applying the conclusions of common experience to new social situations.

A curious standard of values is revealed. Co-operation can only take place between men, society can only exist at all, if certain principles are applied. It becomes entirely unworkable if certain other principles (e.g. that each shall be his own judge of his own rights) are applied. Most of those who emerge from our schools are quite incapable of distinguishing between the workable and the unworkable group of principles; the operation, nature, meaning of society has not been brought home. Why should we regard the lack of all knowledge of the mechanism of human society—the nature of which will depend upon the ideas its members apply to it—with such indifference, while we deem it so important to give every child some notion of the mechanism of heavenly bodies, of the movement of the earth round the sun? His ideas about these phenomena are not going to affect them very much. That the earth is as flat as a pancake might be a common idea, and the ships would still navigate. But the common view that foreigners ought not to send us their goods and ought to pay for ours and settle their debts to us in "Money" has put about half the ships of the world out of business and has helped to reduce millions to the miseries of unemployment.

Take the capacity to apply simple logical or arithmetical tests to the policies which the average voter supports. Still is John Citizen profoundly convinced that the only way to ensure peace (though he may also tell you in another mood that peace is an impossible dream) is to be prepared for war—to be sure of having a bigger stick than the others. He simply declines to face what happens if others use the same argument. He is a practical man, and so insists that peace can be secured to two rival parties by the simple process of each being stronger than the other. He applies exactly the same principles to trade. A nation can only be solvent and prosperous if it sells more than it buys—has a favourable balance of trade; if, that is, some other has an unfavourable balance, and is thus *not* solvent. This is our intellectual preparation for the World

Economic Conference, which is to follow the World Disarmament Conference.

John Citizen is aware that police forces do not arrest each other, and that armies do; that an army is the instrument a nation uses to enforce its view in a dispute with another, the instrument, that is, one litigant uses against another, while the police is an instrument of the judge, the law, restraining both litigants alike. Yet he continues to repeat that "we need armies for the same reason that we need police," and that the Pacifist wants us to leave our doors unlocked so that the burglar may enter freely.

In all this you will charge me, I fear, with a reversion to eighteenth-century intellectualism, in supposing that society is based upon some conscious will or contract. The truth is, however, that I assume the contrary. It is just because the unconscious element bulks so largely in our behaviour, just because unexamined impulse plays so large a part therein, that we have to invoke the importance of guiding instinct in some measure by conscious knowledge based upon experience.

I was much struck by a sentence in a book of the late Graham Wallas, who wrote, you will remember, two notable works, one entitled *Human Nature in Politics*, which appeared in 1908, and another which appeared some six years later. In the Preface of this latter book he says that the earlier one "turned into an argument against nineteenth-century intellectualism, and this . . . has turned at times into an argument against certain forms of twentieth-century anti-intellectualism."

The general conclusions to which these observations point is now perhaps sufficiently indicated. They are intended to prompt, not the introduction into the curriculum of new "subjects"—economics, social organization, ethics, internationalism—but such method of teaching all the social sciences, and some subjects not ranked as "social" like mathematics and language, as to give scholars a lively sense (*a*) of the dangerous anti-social side of human nature as well as its great social potentialities; (*b*) of the way in which man has used his intelligence increasingly to shape his impulses to social ends; (*c*) of the essential insecurity, vulnerability, precariousness and imperfection of human society, the fact that man is always experimenting with it, and some of the conclusions to which those experiments of the past and present seem to point; what hope and what warning they embody; and the principles of social action which seem to emerge; and (*d*) to make the whole process a means of developing the skill for seeing the meaning of facts, of drawing the socially useful conclusions from them.

I do not believe that elementary truths in economics need constitute a separate subject any more than it has been necessary to make bacteriology a part of our school curriculum in order to produce a generation of laymen capable of understanding the need of sanitary measures to prevent pestilence. Given an intellectual habit of wanting to understand how things work, rather than a desire to possess erudition, a knowledge of unrelated facts and events—given that way of learning the present subjects of the curriculum it would not be necessary to introduce new ones.

Any detailed illustration would lead us too far: I see anthropology merged into history as part of the story of the way early societies and social rules were formed; as part of the story of how men began to think, which would bring us to include psychology, and that, also, as part of the explanation of man's infinite cruelties, his massacres, torturings, burnings, inquisitions. And in deciding the relative importance of events I would revise rather radically existing scales of value. To an event like the Battle of Waterloo in a history text-book I might give a few lines; but to events like the coming of money, with its consequent mercantilism, to certain steps in the development of law, to the story of the growth of the inductive method of reasoning, to the laws abolishing torture and slavery, to the story of the coming of religious toleration, of the notion of human equality; of democracy; the coming of nationalism—to the part of history which explains these events and helps to make them intelligible to the ordinary mind, I would devote many, many pages.

And finally I would assume that they *can* be made intelligible to the ordinary mind. The task is obviously difficult, but I would act on the faith that it is not impossible; that we can, even by the instrument of the parable, the Robinson Crusoe story of the formation and failure of certain pocket-edition societies, make sufficient of these things intelligible to the minds of children to set up an increasing realization that what they are engaged upon in their education is a preparation for understanding on the one hand themselves, their natures, and on the other their society, the world which later they will have to live in and help to manage.

I find it is a common experience of those who write a book that they only discover after it is over what they have really been trying to say. Looking back on these lectures, I think I see a little more clearly than when I began what it is I have been trying to say. It is this: That the social revolution about which we talk, which so many of us conceive as the transfer of economic power from the few to the many, will be quite ineffective in giving us a more workable and more humane society unless the many are able to achieve a type of understanding which our education has not, I believe, so far helped us very much to develop. For though it may be true to say that knowledge is power, it is not true to say that power is knowledge; and power of itself, for the reasons which I have elaborated in the foregoing lectures, may well become a mere instrument of self-destruction and of self-enslavement. It will certainly so become if it is employed in the way in which power has, in fact, been

wielded in the hands of nationalistically minded
peoples in the recent past. I can imagine the
Capitalist system—a dangerously vague term—
being overthrown, and there being substituted
for it a Socialist or Communist system with
power in the hands of a party genuinely intending
to express "the will of the people." We might
then make two discoveries: the first, that there
was a lack of actual technical knowledge of how
to use the power to readjust certain parts of the
mechanism; of the money apparatus, for instance,
and that until we knew better how money func-
tioned we should be in danger of dislocating the
whole economic apparatus. Our second discovery
might well be that the coercive tendencies
developed by a dictatorship, in the necessarily
large and complex bureaucracy, would, in practice,
tend to inhibit the very qualities most needed for
the development of a co-operative society. A very
able Communist, who had occupied a prominent
position in the Russian banking system, said to
me not long since: "Whenever we had a conference to decide some difficult financial or
economic problem, our decisions were really
dictated by one overwhelming, dominating motive, this motive: What would Moscow like us
to decide? What will be pleasing to the inner
clique?" No wise public opinion, conscious of
what it wants, able to form the basis of a free
society, can grow out of such a situation. Yet a
bad and intolerant public opinion, the sort of
public opinion which gives us a nationalist

Europe, is just as likely as an informed one to arise and impose itself. In Russia we have seen more than once the Governing group plainly obliged to yield to popular clamour, a sort of Communist Jingoism; just as Western governments have had to yield to popular clamour in such instances as the Treaty-making and the claims against Germany. We have seen Russian technicians executed by the dozen at a time when native technicians were so scarce that thousands of foreign ones had to be imported from capitalist countries. We may fairly assume that the native technicians were sacrificed to a momentary popular clamour for scapegoats. Popular clamour needed a victim, someone to be punished, just as certain features of the Treaty were the outcome of a desire to punish Germany. The guilty nation of our democracies is replaced in Russia by the guilty class.

Perhaps even more under Communism than under Capitalism must the multitude have a type of education which will enable them to know what they want, to disentangle one want from another, to know when they are merely feeding a hungry emotion and when pursuing rationally the means to a conscious end; they, too, need not merely to be shown the way out, but some means by which they can recognize it as the way when it is shown them.

Under any system the millions must have that capacity which enables them to judge tendencies, broad issues—"understanding" rather than erudition and knowledge.

It was said of Poincaré that he knew everything and understood nothing; and of Briand that he knew nothing and understood everything. I fear that our education in the past has tended to place knowledge in this sense above understanding. I feel that it is necessary to reverse the emphasis and place understanding before knowledge. For the things which we have to understand are essentially simple and everyday things.

Where does human understanding fail most dangerously? I have suggested that it fails most in the making of certain necessary social adjustments; and that the need of avoiding that failure in the future should guide us in the reshaping of our educational values, to the end that society, like inanimate nature, can be brought under the control of what may yet, let us hope, prove to be "the unconquerable mind of man."

INDEX

America, Presidential Election in, 24, 31

Asquith, H. H., 183

Baldwin, Stanley, 113, 183

Balfour, Lord, 183

Basle Committee, 21

Bass, Professor, 30

Beaverbrook, Lord, 34, 88, 112, 113, 116

Bernhardi, 41

Beveridge, Sir W. H., 15, 20, 21, 23, 49, 113

Blackett, Sir B., 15

Bonar Law, A., 183

Briand, A., 211

British Broadcasting Corporation, 190

Business Education, Conference on, 112

Capitalism, 42, 47, 130, 131, 134, 163, 166, 170, 171, 175

Castlerosse, Lord, 180

Cecil, Lord, 183

Churchill, Winston, 29, 46

Clay, Henry, 15

Cleveland, Grover, 120

Communism, 16, 129, 209, 210

Cosgrave, W. T., 109

Coty, M., 117

Dawes Plan, 45

Debts, War
    See Reparations

Deflation, 16

Déroulede, M., 117

De Valera, E., 82, 83, 84, 86, 87, 88, 94, 109, 110, 118

Disarmament, 116, 195

Dreyfus Case, 120, 122, 125, 199

Dunsany, Lord, 90

Empire Free Trade, 49, 129

Fascism, 129

Fisher, Professor I., 27

Five-Year Plan, 147

Free Trade, 16, 129

Gold Standard, 16

Grey, Lord, 183

Halley Stewart Lecture, 1931, 15

Hearst, Randolph, 34, 35, 117

Henderson, Arthur, 183

Herriot, E., 24

Hitler, A., 41, 111, 117

Hollis, Senator, 36

Home Marketing Board, 168

Hoover, President, 183

Hugenburg, H., 117

Imperial Finance Committee, 40

Inflation, 16

Isvolsky, 43

Keynes, J. M., 15

Kipling, Rudyard, 198

Layton, Sir W., 113

League of Nations, 73, 77, 113, 114, 180, 181, 182, 189, 194

League of Nations, cost of, 47, 177

Lenin, N., 43

Lippman, W., 152

Lloyd George, D., 101, 183

MacDonald, J. Ramsay, 45, 85, 148, 149, 183

Mercantilism, 17

Millevoye, L., 117

Moulton, Professor, 30

Mussolini, Benito, 41, 111

Nationalism, 17, 40, 41, 43
Navy, American, building of, 32, 33
Nazi movement, 118
Nietzsche, 4
Northcliffe, Lord, 189

O'Rahilly, Professor A., 83

Peace Treaties, 178, 180
Plagues, in East, 52–56
Plato, 149
Poincaré, R., 41, 211
Prophylaxis, 54, 63
Protectionism, 16, 17, 81, 129

Reparations, 23, 25, 26, 27, 28, 29, 47–49, 57, 58, 61, 64, 67, 97, 195
Roosevelt, President T., 88
Rothermere, Lord, 116, 180

St. Bartholomew, Massacre of, 124
Salter, Sir A., 15, 113
Simonds, F., 108

Socialism, 16, 43, 129, 130, 134, 163, 164, 165, 166, 171, 176, 209
Soule, G., 153
Spender, J. A., 30
Stamp, Sir Josiah, 15, 19, 113
Stewart, Sir Halley, 20

Taft, W. H., 183
Technocracy, 147, 148, 150, 152, 153, 154
Temperley, H. W. V., 110
Thompson, Mayor W., 199
Treitschke, 41
Trotsky, L. D., 140, 141

Vanderlip, Frank, 35, 36
Versailles, Treaty of, 185

Wales, Prince of, 112, 113, 115
Wallas, Graham, 205
Wilson, President W., 183

Yeats-Brown, Major F., 90

For Product Safety Concerns and Information please contact our EU
representative GPSR@taylorandfrancis.com
Taylor & Francis Verlag GmbH, Kaufingerstraße 24, 80331 München, Germany

www.ingramcontent.com/pod-product-compliance
Lightning Source LLC
Chambersburg PA
CBHW050438280326
41932CB00013BA/2158

9 7 8 1 0 3 2 8 7 8 7 0 6